living
curiously

How to Use Curiosity
to Be Remarkable
and Do Good Stuff

How to Use Curiosity
to Be Remarkable
and Do Good Stuff

Becki Saltzman

Oomau Media, Portland, Oregon 97239

© 2016 All rights reserved.

Front cover design by Patty McNally and graphics by Dino Paul.

Editing and production by Indigo Editing & Publications.

ISBN: 978-0-9890935-6-9

For Stephen, Barkley, and Dane.

Contents

Introduction

From flaming marijuana glass pipe-blowing competitions in Denver to voodoo priest readings in Louisiana to the largest Pray the Gay Away convention in the country, living curiously has taken me to some mind-blowing places. It has carried me around the world, from remote parts of the Great Wall of China to underground hideouts used during the Spanish Inquisition to the ancient ruins of Peru. But don't think for a moment that these adventures are only available to those who travel the world. Living curiously has also dragged me down the street, where I've met grocery store workers who shared their experiences moonlighting as graffiti and beat-box artists, funeral directors who shared new trends and insights in the death industry, and pole dancers who shared stories of cultures about which I had mostly been unaware.

For me, living curiously has made adventures more inspiring and has filled the mundane of my daily life with mystique. In some ways, living curiously reminds me of when I first got glasses and realized that the leaves on the trees actually had crisp edges, when previously I had thought they looked like a Monet painting. Amazing! Living curiously has also given me new angles of understanding, gained by judging compassionately. Like when I realized that the insane woman at my garage sale wasn't a danger to my family but was rather a deadly, diabetic danger to herself…and that the remedy was orange juice. It has revealed powerful insights that give the word *reward* its many meanings in life and in work.

What's in it for you? Living curiously will help you:

- Uncover what you need to know to make better decisions
- Discover misleading blind spots
- Ask better questions
- Find hidden connections that reveal insights
- Generate new ideas
- Live a more fulfilling and adventurous life

Living curiously is an exciting way to live, but as you will see, it is also more important now than ever before.

...

For twenty years while I sold real estate, my car often doubled as a confessional. I admit that the stories could be juicy fun, but they also served a serious purpose. Listening and helping was as much a part of my real estate services as it was a part of my quest to understand the underappreciated role of curiosity in people's lives. I was a not-so-secret curiosity consultant as well as a real estate broker. During this time, I also studied everything I could get my eyeballs on about curiosity and how it relates to judgment, decision making, creativity, sales, and persuasion. In addition to interviewing clients, customers, and coworkers, I tapped my background in behavioral science and interviewed other unconventional thinkers, including scientists, business and religious leaders, musicians, politicians, hospice workers, holocaust survivors, strippers, morticians, teachers, gun dealers, students, psychics, exotic animal collectors, atheists, designers, tattoo artists, witches, drug dealers, policy makers, chefs and bartenders, and many glorious senior citizens.

Hidden behind both unusual and typical job and life titles were remarkable people—often unconventional thinkers—who were benefitting the world in huge and tiny ways. These folks created questions in response to challenges that they had faced, but not ordinary questions—questions that helped them pursue remarkable lives, such as:

- Can we cure diabetes by giving away healthy pet food?
- Is it possible to fund travel adventures by providing teddy bears to hospitals?
- Could breaking rules save a ruler?
- How can you provide good vibes in a coffee cup?
- Do we get what we deserve?
- Can you buy a tractor with a cigar?
- What is a real answer to the question, how could I ever?
- How can I combat boredom by finding the mystique in the mundane of daily life?

I was deeply inspired by these remarkable people. They were insightful. They saw things that others seemed to miss (including me). Like many of us, they wrestled with what to do to create a meaningful life. They asked unusual questions and then answered those questions to ultimately create meaning by doing good stuff. They were able to inspire beneficial change in their own lives and in the lives of others. I wondered how they did it. Curiosity always had a starring role. But did they do something strategically different with curiosity to create these insightful, rewarding, adventurous lives? Was there some kind of curiosity-driven framework that I could learn? If so, was it supported by the behavioral science that I study and love? And, most importantly, could it actually be taught and used to help others be remarkable and do good stuff in the world?

Out of these decades of research and thousands of interactions and interviews, I discovered the Living Curiously Method. It existed before, of course, organically and unidentified. I just noticed the same five steps taken by these remarkable, curiosity-driven people and placed them in a framework for others to learn and follow. I hope it is as profoundly helpful for you as it has been for me and the people I have shared it with so far.

Elevate *Curiosity*

Adventure
That Inspires

Work
That Rewards

Be Remarkable and *Do Good Stuff*

Part I: Elevating Curiosity

“ *Out beyond ideas of wrongdoing and rightdoing,*
There is a field. I'll meet you there. —Rumi

I was nervously standing alone outside the nation's largest Pray the Gay Away convention compound. The organizers didn't exactly call it a Pray the Gay Away convention, but my understanding was that the goal of the convention was for homosexuals, and their spiritual guides, to pray for a heterosexual orientation. What they officially promote is called gay-conversion therapy. I was there to test the most important principle in the Living Curiously Method, elevating curiosity, to see if it would work in personally difficult settings. For me this setting qualified as extremely difficult.

There are five steps in the Living Curiously Method, but elevating curiosity lives outside these five steps. It is the most important and constant exercise that powers all the steps. It is a reordering process that places curiosity ahead of criticism, judgment, fear, and complacency. Placing curiosity first is not the typical default ordering of the human brain. By nature, when we see something that is different from our own beliefs, new things, or things we don't understand, we criticize it, mark it as other, and shut down attempts to be curious about it. Fear also crushes curiosity. It takes work to swap the order so we start with curiosity in new, different, or uncomfortable situations. That reordering was what I was trying to do while standing outside that convention, preparing to enter the huge church compound.

Are there times when you assume you know all you need to know about places you go or people you meet? Do you often feel that no amount of elevating curiosity would provide additional insights or helpful perspectives? That's almost how I felt at the Pray the Gay Away convention, and that's why I knew it would be a good testing ground for me. Could I elevate curiosity and bust my strongly held assumptions? I do not believe in, nor am I in favor of, reparative therapy for sexual orientation. I don't personally find much value in praying. I knew that if I could elevate curiosity at that convention, I'd be able to do it almost anywhere.

Caught between the crowd of protestors, soul savers, and hopeful participants, I wanted to wink to acknowledge my own team among the protestors…and to reassure myself. I didn't wink, but it did take me more than thirty minutes of using my own curiosity hacks before I could go inside. Curiosity hacks are shortcuts, tips, and heuristic tricks to help use curiosity strategically to see and understand things you could otherwise miss. Once you start practicing the foundational strategy for the Living Curiously Method—elevating curiosity—you'll begin to embrace the Living Curiously Lifestyle and develop your own curiosity hacks.

My hacks could also be called triggers, and these are the ones I use the most:

- Mentally conjuring imagery of a dial or switch that places curiosity first
- Creating the motion my thumb and index finger make when turning a dial
- Imagining jumping on a pogo stick (or actually jumping on mine when it's available)
- Asking myself, "What if I'm wrong?"

As I stood outside the convention that day, the legality of these gay-conversion programs had recently been challenged in the courts and highlighted on the news, and I wanted to be curious, as much as I was struggling before going inside. Eventually my triggers worked, and I was able to enter the church compound with curiosity elevated. The insights I gained at the convention were profound.

As I looked for elation in the faces of the men and women fervently praying for a new orientation, most of what I saw was desperation. I do not consider homosexuality an affliction, but for these desperate Christians, I began to understand something

I had not thought of before. It occurred to me that perhaps same-sex attraction, for them, is an affliction similar to how being born with female chromosomes and anatomy is an affliction for those who know they are, in more ways than not, male. I began to think differently about the conflicting choice of an incompatible religion with an undeniable orientation. The stacks of books and DVDs and the prevalence of coaches and counselors inside that convention center helped me understand the enormous business side of the gay-conversion industry. I saw how, for some participants, having a group of like-minded strugglers created a community of acceptance, while for other sufferers, it highlighted a staggering rejection.

I heard specific language that I had heard spoken by dangerously homophobic African leaders on the news. Missionaries did not introduce homosexuality to the African continent, but it became clear that, cloaked in the salve of salvation, they did introduce homophobia. Since the convention, that same homophobic language has been the justification for the leaders of some African countries to suggest that homosexuality be punishable by death. These curious insights finally allowed me to think critically about the fact that, although these types of gay-conversion programs are not innocuous, that doesn't make it clear that they should be illegal for consenting adults whose religious beliefs and sexual orientation are at odds with each other.

What did this curious adventure do for me? It, and many other such adventures, reminded me of the astonishing value of elevating curiosity to gain insights that I would otherwise miss—even when I think that I know most of what I need to know. I was challenged to acknowledge the difference between making criticisms by judging people according to my perspective and experiences (like thinking they're all a bunch of crackpots) and being a critical thinker by analyzing alternatives with an open mind (like realizing that someone might choose a different path because of a love greater than their sexuality). I learned that judging compassionately results in judging more accurately.

I had to be willing to be wrong about the lack of any value in gay-conversion therapy. This allowed me to gain a deeper understanding of how, for some consenting adults, spirituality can be more important than sexuality. Elevating curiosity requires that you're more concerned with getting your life right than not getting it wrong. It channels your curiosity, giving you its greatest power—the ability to see, question, and understand things you could otherwise miss.

Here's a quick success tip: even if the only practice you adopt from this book is elevating curiosity, your life will begin to be remarkable in wildly wonderful ways. Elevating curiosity will move you from *being* inspired to *taking inspired action*.

Mastery of elevating curiosity is not the mission; practice is the mission. The Living Curiously Method may eventually become second nature, but elevating curiosity won't ever be easy. Practice may never make perfect, but it will bring you much closer to fine. How's that for a realistic promise?

Thinking Differently about This and That

Part of fulfilling that realistic promise is preparing you to think a bit differently in order to lubricate your mind for curiosity. Start with these few concepts.

Change versus Beneficial Change

Many types of change are good; the common fear of change is limiting—both of these statements are true. Perhaps that has resulted in the all-too-common rallying cry to change your life and change the world!

Initially, I thought the Method was a step-by-step approach to using curiosity to prepare you to *change* the world. I soon realized I was wrong. It was something different, and this difference turned out to be important. The Living Curiously Method is focused on strategically aiming curiosity at *effective and beneficial change*, instead of *general change*. What's the difference?

> **"** *I guess one person can make a difference. But most of the time, they probably shouldn't.* — MARGE SIMPSON

The difference is in knowing if and when change is beneficial. In Hebrew, the ancient concept of *tikkun olam* refers to humanity's shared responsibility for repairing the world.[1] That's what the Method helps you do. Benefitting, like repairing, requires questioning assumptions in order to arrive at what is truly beneficial versus what is simply change. Tapping a desire to change the world is too often a way to motivate and move without curiously questioning whether there is any meaningful measurement of making stuff better. The desire to change has been used to justify personal, political, and economic action and reaction that has often caused more harm than necessary. By contrast, doing good stuff via the Method helps you strategically apply curiosity to distinguish between change and beneficial change. All repairs require change, but change is not always beneficial.

The benefits of doing good on a small scale often hide in the short term but later prove to be huge, unforeseen, and rippling. There is no beneficial change too small or too large for the Method. Don't dismiss the beneficial change that might start with you. It could prove to be amazing.

Being Compassionate versus Judging Compassionately

Being compassionate is certainly underrated, but it isn't the same as judging compassionately. Judging compassionately implies a level of critical thinking that is central to the Living Curiously Method. It requires a high degree of curiosity about the best way to apply compassion to be beneficial. It gets you closer to solving problems. For example, being compassionate when you are a teacher may mean that you're frustrated that you're not being as effective as you'd like, but you allow a stressed child to sleep during class. Judging compassionately requires you to curiously follow the root of the child's stress in order to see if she needs food or a place to sleep at night so she can succeed in school and break a cycle of poverty.

We may have enough trouble judging ourselves with compassion, let alone judging others compassionately, but doing so can be a step toward beneficial change. Judging compassionately doesn't make you less judgmental as much as it makes you more accurate in your judgments.

" *Do not do unto others as you would that they should do unto you. Their tastes may not be the same.*
—George Bernard Shaw

The Trap of Right and Wrong

Being wrong creates a sneaky feeling that is deviously similar to being right, because when we are wrong, we often think we're right. This makes being curious about what it feels like to be wrong very tricky. How do we recognize wrong when it is disguised in our minds as right? I am wrong a lot…perhaps more than I think I am. You're probably like me, but I could be wrong.

Getting too comfortable with assuming we're right keeps us from developing comfort with being wrong, and this creates problems for us. It's not like there are obvious incentives for being wrong—no rewards, trophies, or medals. Hell, misspelling words in grade school can lead to a stick figure hanging from the gallows. The seduction of being right and discomfort with being wrong are curiosity killers.

The Living Curiously Method gives you the tools (and bravery) to avoid squashing the curiosity necessary to seek an insightful answer to "What if I'm wrong?"

" *Genuine tragedies in the world are not conflicts between right and wrong. They are conflicts between two rights.*
—George Wilhelm Friedrich Hegel, German philosopher

On Being Remarkable

There is no completely right or wrong definition of what it means to be remarkable. It is personal, and yet it's disingenuous to pretend that it has nothing to do with other people. You gotta question when and whether the "don't care what anyone else thinks" mantra should apply. However, remarkability is not the same as just being noticed—that can happen to any attention addict trying too hard to go viral.

The Living Curiously Method is optimized for remarkability that moves beyond a *desire* to make a beneficial difference to actually *doing* it. This is remarkability that lies outside the boundaries of average. This is also—according to Theodore Roosevelt in his 1910 speech, "Citizens in a Republic"—where the credit belongs:

> The credit belongs to the man who is actually in the arena, whose face is marred by dust and sweat and blood; who strives valiantly; who errs, who comes short again and again, because there is no effort without error and short-coming; but who does actually strive to do the deeds, who knows great enthusiasms, the great devotions; who spends himself in a worthy cause; who at the best knows in the end the triumph of high achievement, and who at the worst, if he fails, at least fails while daring greatly, so that his place shall never be with those cold and timid souls who neither know victory nor defeat.

In the context of the Living Curiously Method, remarkability references a kind of unconventional thinking and unique bravery that leaves little doubt that you will risk being revered…and reviled. Dare in the arena. It will be worth it.

Curious about What You'll Learn?

Now that we've covered the basic foundation of beliefs and definitions for the Living Curiously Method, the rest of the book will show you how to prepare yourself for a remarkable life and how to put your plan into action. The rest of Part I will answer the following questions that you might be curious about:

- Why is curiosity so important now?
- How can you use this book?
- Who is the Living Curiously Method *not* for?
- Who is it for?
- What is it good for?

We'll also take a look at:

- A brief history of curiosity
- The case for curiosity

In Part II you will learn the madness before the Method, and then in Part III you will learn the Living Curiously Method and exactly how to use it. In Part IV you can learn how to dive deeper into the Method...if and when you're ready.

Why Is Curiosity So Important Now?

Now is the time to usher in the Age of Curiosity. Gone are the days when access to information was available only to a select and limited few. Experts such as doctors, real estate agents, lawyers, salespeople, and scientists can no longer easily hoard information, make it secret and powerful, and dish it out to us at their discretion in easily digestible chunks. Information is readily available and is flooding us all with data like never before. We are drowning in data. Applying curiosity strategically may be the only way we can avoid being led astray when we're trying to make sense of the treasure trove of accessible information. Our assumptions and biases will be called upon more than ever to act as filters for the overwhelming data deluge. We must be able to summon and act on our curiosity, and it is more critical than ever that we know how to do it.

It may seem that summoning and acting on curiosity is actually easier than before, but there is a dangerous downside to this assumption. Let's say you're wrestling with a disagreement about a topic at dinner. Easy. There is no need to debate. Just set down your glass and search on your device for the answer. However, the internet's power to easily answer questions has a dark side. If we're not careful to recognize the fragility of our curiosity, our easy access to answers can eliminate the information gap that is essential for curiosity to flourish. Curiosity will cease to apply beyond device addiction. Without curiosity, we can assume too soon that with all we know, we know enough. We can search for and access anything—except what isn't there. Only curiosity generates the very questions that inspire the answers we don't yet have access to. Without curiosity, new answers will cease to exist.

How Can You Use This Book?

We are all busy and have limited time to read a book from cover to cover. You can do that with *Living Curiously*, but you will not be shamed if you don't. It's okay—if for now all you do is learn and practice elevating curiosity, you're off to a great start. When you want to delve deeper into defining your remarkability and doing your good stuff, the Method will be waiting for you.

The Method is divided into five steps that are meant to help you use curiosity strategically to achieve your goal of defining and creating your remarkable life. The steps definitely work best when you go through them for the first time in the exact order presented, but I'm not that bossy about it. Alone, each step can help you develop extremely valuable and specific skills. At the start of each step, the main skills will be highlighted, so if you want to grab that lesson and leave the others for later, that's okay as long as you continue to...you know...practice elevating curiosity.

You will find exercises that are sort of lengthy. Don't worry if you only have a chance to sample some of the exercises now and save the rest for another time. It's more important that you don't burn yourself out and that you actually get to work on your remarkability and good-stuff doing. Living curiously is a lifelong practice, and the world needs you.

Who Is It Not For?

Is the Living Curiously Method *not* for you? I know that's a weird question because it might seem negative, but let's face it, we are all too busy to spend time with things that don't provide value to our lives. This question is meant to be positive, and it's meant to save you time. If the Method is not for you, that's cool. Now you know to gift *Living Curiously* to someone for whom it's a better fit.

Here's a handy list of questions to help you know if the Living Curiously Method is *not* for you. If you answer these questions with "yes," I toast you—I'm always looking for an excuse to toast somebody—but the Living Curiously Method is not optimized for you:

- Are you exactly where you want to be in every aspect of your life?
- Are you unwilling to challenge yourself and your world-view?
- Are you unwilling to be hard on your own opinions?
- Are you someone who views the world in black and white, and you want to continue to do so?
- Are you way more concerned with not getting your life wrong than with getting it right?
- Would you choose privacy and obscurity over putting yourself out there to do good stuff in the world?

For those whom the Method is not for, know that you have lots of company. I get it, and I still like you. Many of us may dip our toes gingerly into the murky pond of the gray area, but eventually, only a few of us dive in.

If you feel that you don't have the luxury of engaging your curiosity right now to take action to be remarkable and do good stuff, the Method might be for you, but now might not be the best time in your life to engage with it. When we are sinking in the quicksand of stress is when our judgments get distorted and our insights grow farther out of reach. Even though that may mean you need the Method the most right then, sometimes it's not realistic. In the meantime, practice elevating curiosity and we'll wait for you.

Who Is It For?

> " *All mankind is divided into three classes: those that are immovable, those that are movable, and those that move.*
> —BENJAMIN FRANKLIN

The Living Curiously Method is designed for unconventional thinkers who desire to define and then create a remarkable life — to move beyond being inspired to actually taking inspired action in order to do good stuff. These are also the people who are brave enough to buck convention in order to do their good stuff.

If you're a creator, philanthropist, or entrepreneur with a desire to make and inspire beneficial change, you already possess the chops for this bravery. The Method is probably for you. If you're starting to see how curiosity can uncover insights that you can use to make smarter decisions—yep, you guessed it—you're on the right track. If you can envision the value of curiosity to create adventure that inspires and work that rewards, forge ahead. If you're truly curious about how to understand, convince, persuade, or better relate to your partner, spouse, family members, friends, neighbors—and even your boss or employees—in order to work toward doing good in the world, this will work for you. If you acknowledge that what you see isn't all that there is, and you're ready to remove what may be blocking you from getting the life you want, you're a perfect fit.

To let you in on a little secret, here is *when* it's best for: when what you think you know about your life collides with the pesky truth of reality...and you're willing to invite in curiosity.

What Is It Good For?

" *While we are postponing, life speeds by.* —Lucius Seneca

The road from inspiration to inspired action is paved with curiosity. *Living Curiously* reveals the Method that will show you how to strategically harness and use curiosity about yourself and others to make and inspire beneficial change. It can also help you bust through three stagnations—idea stagnation, viewpoint stagnation, and life stagnation—that may be blocking you from being highly effective and making a difference in the world. It can act like a machete cutting through thorny thickets of your life when:

- You want to capture the greatest power of curiosity to solve problems in unusual ways, create fun puzzles out of complex issues, interact with diverse people in interesting places with greater understanding, and have more fun and adventure...in order to do good stuff

- You hold a burning desire to share your knowledge and talents in order to have tremendous impact in life, in business, in philanthropic endeavors, or on your friends and family
- You want your success to be a result of helping others succeed
- You absolutely must design and create your own bigger, more meaningful, and inspiring life, adventures, and work
- You're ready to experience richness in every sense of the word…in order to do good stuff

Although the Living Curiously Method is really a framework of systematic curiosity hacks for your life, it is also excellent as a business tool. If you create work that rewards, you will want your inspired life to feed your rewarding work—and vice versa. If you have enjoyed major success contributing to your worthy organization and want to be a lead character in the next generation of success stories, the Method will help you win that leading role. Curiosity will help you lead because you'll see things that other people won't. Your journey or project will be directed using the Method.

The Living Curiously Method is also designed as a critical thinking, judgment, and decision-making tool. This is vital for your endeavors to do good stuff. Although the Method is deeply rooted in sexy mind science—particularly judgment, decision making, and persuasion—this book is not overly academic. I recognize that we are busy and buried in data like never before. Academia is great for longer ponderings, and while I include the Brief History of Curiosity and some exploration into cognitive biases for nerding out, I want to keep you close to your own key questions: What does this mean? What does this mean for me? Is it for me? Only when those questions are in focus can you begin to apply the Method in order to work your magic on the bigger issues.

This is the point when, if you aren't getting excited, the skepticism may be creeping in. Bring on the snarky. That's okay. Actually, it's better than okay—it's perfect. Although it works for optimists, occasional doubters, and frequent skeptics, as you now know, the Living Curiously Method is absolutely not suited for everybody.

❝ *Common sense is the collection of prejudices acquired by age eighteen.* —ALBERT EINSTEIN

History's curiosity seekers were often faced with skepticism too.

A Brief History of Curiosity

If you're not curious about the history of curiosity, that's okay—skip it for now. A brief recap of a long history of curiosity makes it clear that even before it was accused of killing the cat, curiosity was not always perceived as a good thing. Curiosity is, and always has been, more controversial and complex than it seems. As nonconformists, that's one of the things that entices us, right?

Let's start back with the old-timey philosophers. Many call Aristotle Plato's top student and the first real scientist in history. As inquisitive as Ari was, he was not a lover of curiosity. Science-y Aristotle actually dismissed curiosity while singing the praises of wonder. We may think, *What's the difference?* but Aristotle thought that curiosity was an aimless, prying waste of time and that wonder was the true root of inquiry and philosophy.

Until the seventeenth century, most people agreed with Aristotle on that particular point, and curiosity was frowned upon as both a frivolous pursuit and a dangerous and reviled search into what we have no business knowing. This made Aristotle a good boy in the church's eyeball (which was perhaps the point of the distinction between curiosity and wonder) because early Christianity not only frowned upon curiosity but also actually considered it a big old sin.

The early Christian church particularly frowned upon the type of curious inquiry sought by mixing knowledge from a wide array of people, which the Method calls cross-pollinating, rather than from a similar group of intellectual elites. Knowledge that was hoarded by the intellectual elite was considered more important than the knowledge that just anyone could obtain by curious inquiry. Curiosity that explored and exposed the lay knowledge of the makers (farmers, workers, craftspeople) was flat-out condemned. The Middle Ages could be seen as the

Anti-Cross-Pollination Ages, with the emphasis on valuing scholastic knowledge that had been vetted through the ages. This created a caste system of information hoarding. It was like an old-timey version of more recent times, like before the World Wide Web, when information used to be far less accessible to all of us. Back then, the hoarders of information used their elite opportunity to hurl accusations of heresy at those who defiantly embraced curiosity. "Burn them at the stake!"[2]

> **"** *It is the mark of an educated man to be able to entertain a thought without accepting it.* —Aristotle

There have been a lot of amazing philosophers, but Galileo deserves a special prize, and if I could posthumously induct him into the Tribe of the Curious,[3] I would. In addition to donning those jaunty Renaissance-y outfits in the Italian style, he played a major role in the scientific revolution to which we should all be grateful. His tweaking and improving upon early telescopes allowed him to study the stars. He shocked the church with his public and blasphemous claims that the Earth revolves around the Sun instead of the other way around. His controversial approach to curiosity marked a shift away from esotericism and hoarding secrets, toward applying the knowledge derived from curiosity for the good of humanity. Perhaps the Indigo Girls' song "Galileo" could play during his induction ceremony into the Tribe of the Curious. After all, they were the ones who deemed him the "king of night vision" and "king of insight."

> **"** *Galileo's head was on the block*
> *The crime was looking up the truth*
> —Indigo Girls

Francis Bacon was a contemporary of Galileo, and although he did not share Galileo's stargazing abilities, Bacon was perhaps the first scientist to point out the danger of our thinking that we're each the star in the center of our own universe. He sounded the alarm regarding the dangers in judgment caused by cognitive biases. Cognitive biases are crazy gifts that, as human brain owners, we have all received. They're comfortable patterns of questionable judgment that often lead to poor decision making. Our biases are sneaky and hide in plain sight, so we often don't even know they are there. Francis warned that our curiosity should extend beyond judging everything from our own human perspective if we want to make accurate judgments.

Francis was a fluffy-collared, Renaissance English philosopher, statesman, scientist, orator, author, and jurist who has been credited with focusing curiosity directly on things that create useful knowledge. He was a proponent of using curiosity strategically. His pursuits were not just about curiously uncovering natural laws but rather also about applying experimental manipulations to solve complex puzzles. Francis too could be posthumously inducted into the Tribe of the Curious.

" *The human understanding when it has once adopted an opinion (either as being the received opinion or as being agreeable to itself) draws all things else to support and agree with it.*
—FRANCIS BACON

Francis called for an official place to collect and promote knowledge derived from observation. Thus, in the mid-1600s, a group of physicians, philosophers, and other great thinkers started the Royal Society[4] to gather together and follow their curiosity by conducting scientific experiments—some of the earliest on record. The idea was to promote the knowledge of the natural world through observation and experiment.

Within what could now be considered the broad realms of science and philosophy, the Royal Society drew from a wide variety of academic disciplines. The insights they obtained by mixing and mingling across different disciplines back in the day should provide a takeaway lesson in cross-pollination for us today. In our world of hyperspecialization, it will be increasingly important to stretch our curiosity muscles to look outside of and beyond our specialties—to cross-pollinate.

One of the coolest things about the Royal Society has to be its collection of natural rarities and curiosities. This idea of a cabinet of curiosities was popularized in the sixteenth century as a way to spark curiosity and intrigue about strange and unusual objects of nature. I'd ignore my claustrophobia and rustle around in the Royal Society's cabinets of curiosities any day. The society still exists, so maybe someday I'll get my chance.

> **"**Nullius in verba.
> —ROYAL SOCIETY MOTTO,
> LATIN FOR "TAKE NOBODY'S WORD FOR IT."

There are still remnants of the time when curiosity was condemned as dangerous and blasphemous. The negative connotation of the word *heretic* still exists even though a heretic might be more aptly defined as a nonconformist. Three cheers for us heretics! The word *occult* innocently denotes that which is beyond the range of knowledge or understanding, yet the word also suffers from a negative connotation as something dangerous and wrong—as many cults, like the Movement for the Restoration of the Ten Commandments of God[5] and Children of the God[6] have been.

At the Royal Society, adventure and conquests were often synonymous with curiosity quests. Members circumnavigated the globe and brought curiosities back to the society and royal courts to study and store them. The movement of the planets was of particular interest and aroused the curiosity of early astronomers. They were among the first to try to predict the future with an applied science.

Instruments such as the telescope and microscope provided a way of investigating beyond the capabilities of the naked eye. Some early skeptics questioned whether and how those instruments could be trusted. Should we be equally skeptical of today's tools for analyzing big data?

Space exploration has always been associated with curiosity. In 2011 the car-sized robot named *Curiosity* was sent to Mars in what today looks to be a one-way ticket, with the goal of assessing Martian climate and geology. Curious about living on Mars? NASA recently reported that Curiosity (aka the Mars rover) will now be searching for ancient life and evidence of habitability.

What does modern science say about what arouses our curiosity? In the mid-1960s, Daniel Berlyne, a psychologist at the University of Toronto, suggested that curiosity is aroused when we encounter uncertainty or ambiguity in our environment. Later, Carnegie Mellon psychologist George Loewenstein tweaked this to the more buzz-phrase-y term *information gap*.[7] He described this as the gap between some desired knowledge and our existing information set. Perhaps this info gap is what makes a person with a New Year's resolution to work out click on a link when he sees click bait like, "Click here to find why trainers hate this insanely buff guy!"

Berlyne believed that curiosity is a natural human drive and therefore, when new information doesn't jibe with our old information, we react with curiosity.[8] The problem with this statement is that there is a lot of stuff we don't know, and we often don't act with curiosity when we encounter the unknown. Cognitive biases get in our way and can act like invisibility cloaks, shielding us from knowing *what* we don't know...and even shielding us from knowing *that* we don't know. It is not pathetic to admit that this can be exhausting. We are busy.

Recently, Loewenstein and his colleague Russell Golman created a new model designed to understand and capture what makes us want to strive for new knowledge.[9] They found that we seek information we like thinking about and reject information we don't like thinking about (an "ostrich effect," because we stick our heads in the sand when we don't want to think about something).

So the information gap has to be relevant to us in order for us to want to take significant time to fill it. The more relevant the information gap, the more likely you are to be curious. As in the earlier click-bait example, you may not care to click to find out about muscle gain if you don't care about getting buff.

Imagine that the one person whom you really wish you could understand but never have been able to is handing you a piece of paper with the words *If you only knew* written mysteriously and without further explanation. A gap?

Or to get even more obvious, let's say you never cared that you don't know much about human bones until you dig up a box of them in your yard...or discover that you have a bone disease.

In writing *Living Curiously*, I have challenged myself to figure out how to spark a sense of the right kind of relevance to the right people (you?) to make it applicable and spreadable. Most importantly I want it to help you be amazingly successful at solving the challenges that stand in the way of your enjoying a remarkably rewarding life of adventure and doing good in the world. Assuming we are the ones who have chosen to embrace curiosity, the fun and value of this whole adventure is to take a page out of Francis Bacon's book and strategically tap into curiosity in order to do something useful with it.

The Case for Curiosity

“*Only those who will risk going too far can possibly find out how far one can go.* —T. S. ELIOT

Curiosity's reputation, like all of ours (okay, like mine), is not completely untarnished. It's complicated. Curiosity has been credited with going too far (promiscuity—probably not what T. S. was referring to in the quote above, but maybe), trying too many things (drug use), risking too much (winning a Darwin Award), and "just seeing if it would burn" (arson).

Curiosity can be sexy, helpful, and glorious. It comes naturally to some, is more challenging to others, and is forbidden by many. Curiosity causes happiness and excitement when it increases stimulation, fosters exploration, and reduces tension—like when you find what you're looking for.

Even when it gets us into trouble, the curious anticipation of acquiring knowledge is one of the most pleasurable aspects of curiosity. Curiosity can also cause frustration and deprivation when we don't have access to new or desired information— like when we've almost solved a complex riddle or we're trying to figure out why someone dumped us.

Does curiosity's conflicted reputation make it more appealing, or is the positive kind of curiosity actually of a different nature? Is there really good and bad curiosity?

Perhaps the power of curiosity comes from its complexity. Harnessing that power requires you to choose to channel it strategically, and that's what the Living Curiously Method helps you do.

If not channeled properly, curiosity can create a mental spin cycle. Jumping from question to question without any attempt to form a deeper understanding, delving into things that are none of our business for ill intent, or dispassionately pursuing knowledge to be squirrelled away in order to appear smarter than others are not the ways curiosity works in the Living Curiously Method.

The Method works by aiming curiosity as you move through the steps. This suggests a purpose that will take you into the unplanned fun of curiosity, and then deeper to where curiosity's strategic value is astonishingly clear.

Living curiously is not about endless inquiry. It is about uncovering what you need to know to make better decisions, solve problems, and live a more fulfilling and adventurous life.

“*I have no special talents. I am only passionately curious.... The important thing is not to stop questioning. Curiosity has its own reason for existing. One cannot help but be in awe when one contemplates the mysteries of eternity, of life, of the marvelous structure of reality. It is enough if one tries merely to comprehend a little of this mystery every day. Never lose a holy curiosity.* —ALBERT EINSTEIN*

Part II: The Madness Before the Method

Do you want to be just a wee bit more prepared for getting the most out of the Method? If so, here you go. Grab a few more curiosity hacks, and I'll share a bit more about my own story in order to show you how powerfully helpful the Method can be. Finally, you will begin to set a vision—either blurry or clear—for what your goals might be, so you can focus on them as you make your way through the Method's steps for the first time.

More Curiosity Hacks (and an Invitation)

As we set the stage for your great things to come, in addition to remembering to elevate curiosity, there are a few other curiosity hacks that will prepare you to launch the Method. Here are some of them…and they come with an invitation.

Remove the Rhetorical

> *How can we ever? Why would anyone? Why would I? How can I? Should I wash it first?* —THINGS WE ASK FLIPPANTLY

Ask questions like you want a real answer. Removing the rhetorical aspect of commonly asked questions makes the questions more valuable and worthy of answers. Swapping judgment with curiosity while removing the rhetorical aspects of these questions reveals important insights. You may just get amazingly surprising answers.

A genuine answer to the question you might ask a coworker, "Why is my boss such an asshole?" can be a valuable bonding opportunity if you are really curious about the answer and you find out that you and your boss are both going through a divorce or dealing with a child with a serious illness. The answer to "How would I ever leave my job and start a new career or travel the world when I don't have the luxury of a trust fund?" may be vital to being able to accomplish those things. The answer to "How can I get along with my in-laws when we just don't relate (or they just don't like me)?" can save your marriage...and your sanity. The answer to, "Why is my daughter suddenly acting psychotic?" can save her life.[10]

" *When you change the way you look at things, the things you look at change.* —MAX PLANCK, FATHER OF QUANTUM PHYSICS

Bravely Question an Assumption or Two

The Living Curiously Method does not require you to have been born curious, nor do you have to start out insanely curious, but it works well if you were and are. Perhaps your curiosity has been stifled by a didactic education or seductive faith. The Method will not just teach you to be curious—it will also teach you to use your curiosity in a very specific and actionable way. You don't need to jump a motorcycle across the Grand Canyon or travel around the world, but it's cool if you want to. The Living Curiously Method can enhance those supersized adventures too. To start, all you have to do is be just curious and brave enough to wonder if some of your assumptions are worthy of reconsideration. As a warm-up, pick two of your very own assumptions to question. For example, you could think about questioning your assumption that your chosen political party has the best ideas about addressing terrorism or income disparity or health care. Give yourself two bonus points if you try doing this during an election year.

You don't have to question everything. You will actually have an opportunity to choose which of your assumptions you hold too sacred to question. Simply acknowledging and identifying the assumptions you refuse to question helps reduce the risk of them leading you astray, but the more assumptions you question, the more benefits you'll see.

> **"**
> *You act like mortals in all that you fear, and like immortals in all that you desire.... How late it is to begin really to live just when life must end! How stupid to forget our mortality, and put off sensible plans to our fiftieth and sixtieth years, aiming to begin life from a point at which few have arrived!*
> —Lucius Seneca

Your Invitation: Join the Tribe of the Curious

My dream is for the Living Curiously Method to help you and other unconventional thinkers create your own Living Curiously Lifestyle, and then teach others to do the same. I invite you join the Tribe of the Curious at www.LivingCuriously.net. My fantasy is that the tribe becomes a force for solving challenging problems and creating a new way to view the world. It will welcome dissention and controversy. Skeptics and seekers will sit together at the head of the table, while humorists will pour cocktails down their gullets and shirts. People who value happiness and positive thinking will cross-pollinate with people who value snarkiness and cynical humor. Scientists will roll their eyes while finding just enough value to simultaneously raise their eyebrows. All of this will be done in the service of benefitting the world.

> **"**
> *Curiosity...is the lust of the mind.* —Thomas Hobbes

The Method in My Own Life

Before jumping into the Method, I want to share two personal stories that represent curiosity as an early star and a lifesaver in my own life.

Can You Buy a Tractor with a Cigar?

Fostering curiosity in our children is vital to our society's future, and perhaps there are no better people to do that than unconventional thinkers and curiosity seekers (like you?). I think it was the unconventional part of my early upbringing that initially fostered curiosity in me. Before I ever read books or studies[11] on the proven importance of curiosity to learning, my remarkably unconventional parents already knew to create information gaps that inspired curiosity with unusual questions like: "Can you buy a tractor with a cigar?"

Being challenged to seek an answer to that question, and to questions like it, started when I was six years old and my parents cut my hair, dressed me as a boy, and dragged me to what would be my first of hundreds of dusty industrial auctions. They wanted me to learn the family auction business and the art of selling from the master auctioneers. My mom promised that I would grow to love that "pixie hairdo." It took several decades, but eventually she was right. Looking back, it's clear to me that this experience and others like it have helped me establish a lifestyle of living curiously.

Why did they dress me up as a boy? The industrial auction world was filled with grease, heavy equipment, and lots of off-color joking and swearing. I loved it, but as annoying and sexist as it was, and probably still is, the presence of a girl would have changed the dynamic. They wanted me to have a different perspective, and I was game.

What about curiosity? The auctions were full of interesting people, unusual contraptions, and amazing psychology. Passive observation was not enough, and I was constantly challenged to elevate curiosity and question my own assumptions. I was challenged to recognize what I was missing—and I usually missed a lot. On the way home from auctions, I was quizzed with questions like:

- Why does every auction start with a wrench? It was the auctioneer's trademark, and his way of getting people used to bidding by starting with a commonly useful and inexpensive item.
- Why did the auctioneer race through some expensive items, giving bidders very little time to decide, and do the opposite with items of similar value? He was creating an atmosphere of unpredictable excitement and scarcity.
- Why does it look like the auctioneer is calling plays like a football coach to his spotters in the crowd? He is creating drama and providing social proof that a lot of people are participating and bidding.

- Why was that man tipping his cigar up and down during the bidding for that big tractor? That was how the man secretly bids without his competitors knowing and deviously bidding him up.
- Who is that guy that you see at every auction, and why is he always dressed so differently that it's hard to recognize him? He doesn't want his competitors to easily recognize him, know what he's buying, and bid him up.
- Would you be surprised to learn that man in the fancy car works for the guy in the dirty overalls? This was an early lesson that taught me that what you see is never all that there is.
- What does that huge machine do? I may think that all the machines look like big, greasy beasts, but many people find that the subtle differences in each machine are the reason they're in business … and spending hundreds of thousands of dollars at the auction.

That last question always stumped me, and it continues to stump me. Perhaps I was less curious about the function of the specific items being sold and was more curious about the psychology of selling. To this day, I would probably overpay for a large-log cable lifter and never know it, but whether I'm at a fancy art auction or a dusty industrial auction, I'm aware of the microexpressions and movements that can become a winning bid—including a tip of a cigar.

> **"** *If you can light the spark of curiosity in a child, they will learn without any further assistance, very often…. Curiosity is the engine of achievement.* —Sir Ken Robinson

As I learned in my cross-dressing childhood, curiosity plays a starring role in learning and creating awareness of what you may be missing. What I learned in those greasy warehouses when I was six, I confirmed in the dusty halls of academia as a graduate student in psychology working on a mathematical model of behavioral science. I went on to apply those techniques as I built the kind of successful real estate career that focused on beneficially changing people's lives…while they beneficially changed mine.

With time, I witnessed that the power and importance of elevating curiosity in life-and-death decision making is even more dramatic.

How Does a Curiosity Hack Matter When It Comes to Life and Death?

As I was winding down my wonderful career in real estate, my mom, Carol, was diagnosed with brain cancer. I used our last months together to discuss and promise to fulfill my plans to share this Living Curiously Lifestyle and Method, and to acknowledge the fact that she would never appreciate my choices of travel destinations…or lipstick colors. Although curiosity did not save her life, it directed her to ask the kinds of curious questions that allowed her to design her own dignified death.

Then, during my very last days in real estate, as I was getting ready to launch my first book, *Arousing the Buy Curious*,[12] my oldest teenage son, Barkley, was diagnosed with cancer. Although I'm tempted to say that the curiosity hack of elevating curiosity saved my son's life, that's too hard to prove. I'll let you be the judge.

Remaining curious in the face of panic is hard when all we want is a quick salve of calm to reduce the panic. This was all too salient to me, having just lost my mother within months of my son's diagnosis. When faced with a serious medical issue, we are told to be curious in a very specific way—essentially to slow down, remain curious, and get a second opinion—that can be at odds with our need for a quick reduction of panic. It makes perfect sense and sounds like a logical suggestion, but curiously enough, the vast majority of us do not seek second opinions… unless we're doctors.

We avoid second opinions because we feel guilty for cheating on our doctor, we feel comfortable with our doctor, we think it will make our doctor mad, we can't afford it, we're busy, or we're scared. Often our first opinion gives us exactly what we want to hear so we are…done. Generally, we obtain second opinions only when our insurance requires it, when we're not comfortable with our doctor, when we're mad at our doctor, or when we're not comfortable with what we learned. In times of extreme stress, comfort can kill our curiosity.

Although I'm a research maniac, having just gone through my mother's cancer journey and those of several of my friends, my emotions were still very raw and had an impact on my decision-making ability. I was aware of the negative effect that fear can have on good decision making and, frankly, I was terrified. I didn't want fear to get in the way of curiosity and lead me to make bad decisions, so I tried to elevate curiosity and encouraged those around me to do the same. I didn't realize until later how important it would be for them to remind me of this curiosity hack when I was faltering.

I researched the best surgeons, endocrinologists, oncologists, and radiologists for my son's treatment, and we made an appointment with a highly respected surgeon immediately. I also scheduled an appointment with a second highly respected surgeon for a few days later. He was unable to see us sooner.

When we met with the first talented surgeon, my husband, son, and I felt a tremendous relief. We felt reassured by the competence of the doctor, her degree from one of the top medical centers in the country, the prognosis she gave, and the fact that she agreed with a series of presurgery tests recommended by our highly regarded oncologist. A scary burden had been lifted, and we immediately scheduled the surgery for the next week. We felt comfortable with the doctor's views on childhood cancer because they matched our own views. In our minds, her strong credentials reinforced her treatment plan.

We didn't know it yet, but we had viewpoint stagnation. We were all so relieved that we were ready to cancel the appointment for the second opinion. Deep down, I was more afraid than I would admit that the second doctor would challenge our calm and snatch away the temporary relief the first doctor had given us. I was looking for a quick fix, which made me want to cancel the second opinion at the exact moment when our brains were calm and receptive enough to properly evaluate that second opinion and compare it to the first. We all felt similarly. We were all less curious.

Thankfully my younger son, Dane, asked, "I thought it was always good to get a second opinion. Should we really cancel the second doctor's appointment?" The idea of elevating curiosity had been drilled into his skull from an early age. At first I tried to justify canceling. In doing so, I failed to elevate curiosity when it came to assessing and answering my son's critical question. Instead of immediately stopping to think and admit out loud that the comforting prognosis and quickly determined protocol should be questioned, at least minimally, I jumped right into justification mode. I argued that we could have Barkley's cancer out faster if we stuck to the newly scheduled surgery and didn't wait for a second opinion. That seemed fair. From there I jumped right into criticism by pointing out that, unlike the first doctor we saw, the second doctor wouldn't move his schedule around to see us right away, so perhaps he was less caring. I made us all acknowledge that it sure felt good and right when we had booked the surgery. That was when my wise husband, Stephen, reminded me that we needed to elevate curiosity in order to avoid taking this dangerous shortcut.

With that, I realized that once we felt less afraid, we no longer wanted to seek a second opinion because we were not looking to reignite our fear. We wanted to allow criticism (the second doctor is less caring because he didn't accommodate us faster) and justification (we can have the cancer out faster if we stick to the quickly scheduled surgery) to replace our curiosity. At the exact time when we were in a calmer mental state to compare, contrast, and evaluate opinions, we wanted to shortcut the process.

We were falling victim to the affect heuristic. Daniel Kahneman, author of *Thinking, Fast and Slow* and winner of the Nobel Prize in economics, described the way many people make decisions as examples of the affect heuristic.[13] It's a mind trick that shortcuts the judgment and decision-making process, allowing our feelings of like and dislike to lure us without curious deliberation or reasoning. When we're faced with a difficult question, we often answer a slightly different and easier question instead, without noticing that we made a sneaky substitution. I did this when faced with my son's cancer diagnosis, and I initially evaluated the doctor on how well we liked her and how calm she made us feel, instead of whether her protocol was the smartest.

Thankfully the affect heuristic did not prevent us from keeping the appointment for the second opinion. The second surgeon was hesitant to criticize another doctor's recommendations, but because our son's life was at stake, he did. He explained to us that one of the presurgery tests our oncologist had scheduled and the first surgeon supported would have made our son's postsurgery radiation treatment potentially ineffective. It was scary to read about different outcomes and different protocols for treatment, but we tried not to allow fear to get in the way of our curiosity. In the diminishing haze of panic, we were able to properly evaluate our options—and two different protocols. The protocol suggested by the second doctor appeared to have a significantly higher rate of effectiveness than that of the first doctor. It certainly worked well for our son. Upon further research, it could be said that elevating curiosity above fear, criticism, and justification saved our son's life.

Although the curiosity hack of elevating curiosity is a way of life for me (as I hope it will be for you), it is clear that I have not achieved mastery. I doubt I ever will. This is why it is critical to surround ourselves with others who have embraced this Living Curiously Lifestyle to help us when we need it most; this is yet another reason why I encourage you to join the Tribe of the Curious.[14] We need each other.

The Good Stuff You'll Do

I hope by now you are starting to have more of a crush on curiosity. It's time to sharpen your focus on doing the good stuff. What good stuff will you do?

Whether your idea is crisp or vague, that's okay. The Method is meant to help you identify and set goals for your remarkable life. Here are some ideas to get your goal-setting juices flowing:

- Preparing to travel to a foreign country to get inspiration for doing good stuff in the world
- Addressing a family feud involving politics
- Living a more adventurous life
- Being recognized as a leader at work to contribute more effectively
- Making a personal life change with regard to career or marital status

- Launching a new career
- Writing a book
- Helping your students think critically
- Starting a charity
- Creating a system for reducing racial, gender, sexual, economic, or political divisiveness
- Building a successful real estate career to help more people successfully experience home ownership
- Helping your family or friend navigate a crisis
- Raising curious kids
- Helping your newly graduated daughter or son choose the right path for her or him
- Figuring out what philanthropic project to get involved with
- Finding a new way to look at what's working and not working for you with online dating
- Enhancing your coaching career
- Becoming a medical advocate for an ill friend or family member
- Meeting new people in a new city who want to work to heal the world
- Creating a health and fitness program
- Deciding which assumptions you're willing to question that may be limiting you
- Inspiring others to make sense of their complicated lives
- Figuring out how to actively design the rest of your life
- Tackling an audacious global challenge
- Sharing your talents with a greater audience
- Figuring out what quest might be right for you
- Falling back in love with your life in order to help others do the same

Write down your goal(s) for doing good stuff. I like using a number two pencil on a Post-It Note because I can stick it on the bathroom mirror and erase and tweak as necessary. My second best ideas come to me in the shower, right by that note. You can do it however you want, but do write down your initial goal(s). Now you're ready.

Part III: The Living Curiously Method

The Living Curiously Method is a structured, step-by-step framework that will show you exactly how to use curiosity strategically to define and then create your remarkable life in order to do good stuff in the world. Additional benefits are that you will create and experience adventure that inspires and work that rewards. It continuously challenges you to activate and elevate curiosity as you prepare and propel yourself.

Is It for Life or for Work?

> " *A master in the art of living draws no sharp distinction between his work and his play, his labour and his leisure, his mind and his body, his education and his recreation. He hardly knows which is which. He simply pursues his vision of excellence through whatever he is doing and leaves others to determine whether he is working or playing. To himself he always seems to be doing both. Enough for him that he does it well.*
> —Lawrence Pearsall Jacks

The Living Curiously Method works for creating the kind of remarkable life and beneficial change that can end up in your eulogy or on your resume—it's for both life and work. If you choose to embrace the Method for life *or* work, that works too. I admit I could be wrong and ignorant to not specifically choose to define the Method as being a better tool for life instead of for work or vice versa. As Richard Saul Wurman, the founder of the

TED conferences, said, "I worship at the foot of my ignorance. I am so proud to be more ignorant than anybody else in this room. The terror, the absolute terror of not knowing is my friend and comfort is not my friend." So let's wink at ignorance and drink to curiosity. Bottoms up.

5 Steps for Your Living Curiously Remarkable Self

❝ *Try to keep your mind open to possibilities and your mouth closed on matters that you don't know about. Limit your 'always' and your 'nevers.'* — AMY POEHLER

The Living Curiously Method is broken into five steps best followed in sequence:

1. Start with What You're Not
2. Dumpster-Dive Your Life
3. Cross-Pollinate
4. Find Uncommon Commonalities
5. BLAST

The primary benefit of each step will be identified at the start of each one, so after going through the Method, you can revisit them to polish up a step from time to time. The first two steps involve the internal investigation that requires you to become curious about yourself in very specific and tactical ways. It's hard to define and create a remarkable life with a purpose to help and inspire others if you're not curious about yourself first. The second two steps involve an external investigation that requires you to strategically follow your curiosity about others. These first four steps are the preparation for taking the fifth step.

The fifth and final step is the call to action. Philosophical exercises in curiosity (like Curiosity Bites found at www.Living Curiously.net) are great primers. They create fun party discussions and inspire insightful business summits, but the Living Curiously Method is not just a philosophical exercise. You'll actually do stuff. Some fun stuff. Some provocative stuff. All stuff that will help you build upon tactical curiosity about yourself and strategic curiosity about others in order to solve real problems.

You'll start to recognize it. Curiosity builds on itself. Throughout *Living Curiously*, you'll tackle exercises designed to get you thinking differently, to lubricate your mind for curiosity. Some exercises will be more reflective, and others will be more action oriented. There is not a crisp division between the purposes of the exercises, but they are broken into three primary types:

- Lubrication: These will prepare (lubricate) your mind for curiosity.
- Reflection: These tend to be a bit more personal. They will help you answer the question: What does this mean for me?
- Propulsion: These will pull together all the information you gathered and move you to take action toward your goal.

You're ready. Now on to the Method.

Step 1: Start with What You're Not

❝ *You have enemies? Good. That means you've stood up for something, sometime in your life.* —Winston Churchill

What does starting with what you're not have to do with curiosity? Beautiful question.

❝ *Always the beautiful answer who asks a more beautiful question.* —E. E. cummings

What's the best way to know what you don't know? How often do you curiously assess what you don't know without inviting stifling self-criticism? How often do you assess what you don't stand for or who is not your optimal audience *before* others decide for you? Questioning, identifying, and then understanding what we're not requires and inspires great curiosity. We often fail to ask ourselves the questions that start this process because this type of curiosity can be stressful. It focuses on the two stages of Step 1 of the Method:

1. Identify what you *don't know*. This means what you don't know...yet.

2. Identify what you are *not for*. This means both what you don't stand for, and whom you're not trying to reach (your "nonaudience").

Facing this curiosity takes action and a certain amount of bravery. It also enhances your curiosity as you make your way through Step 1 of the Method.

Don't get me wrong—Step 1 is fun, but it can be unpleasant. It's like realizing that with all the work you're doing to combat climate change, you recognize that you *don't know* about the differences between potentially contributing factors like water vapor, carbon dioxide, methane, nitrous oxide, and chlorofluorocarbons. In this example, *you do not stand for* denying something exists just because you don't understand all the hidden science behind it. Also, *you are not targeting* people deeply rooted in the molecular science of climate change.

Living curiously is not about endless inquiry and waiting for the unattainable goal of knowing everything. It is about being curiously vigilant about knowing enough to make better decisions, solve problems, and live a more fulfilling and adventurous life.

Identify What You Don't Know

Remember that this is what you don't know...*yet*. It can be more painful than a poke in the eyeball, but it is amazing how much you learn and how brave you become when you acknowledge what you don't know. Identifying what you don't know helps you usefully and strategically question assumptions that stand as secret roadblocks to beneficial change. Plant a wet kiss on yourself for being willing to explore and acknowledge what you don't know—it's powerfully good of you.

Key Benefits

There are three key benefits to identifying what you don't know:

- Revealing gaps in your knowledge...so you can fill them or decide not to
- Becoming comfortable with not knowing
- Crisping up your goal and your message

Revealing Gaps in Your Knowledge…So You Can Fill Them or Decide Not To

It's hard to know what you don't know. It's even hard to know *that* you don't know. This becomes even more complicated when there are a lot of things that you do know that may be misleading. For example, people who invested with Bernie Madoff absolutely knew he was a successful financial guy, a former chairperson of NASDAQ, a generous philanthropist, and loyal family man. However, none of this made him trustworthy enough not to cheat his Ponzi scheme victims out of more than $50 billion. Had someone used curiosity to identify the gaps in their knowledge about Madoff, maybe the scheme would have tailspinned sooner.

To the extent that what you don't know relates to the remarkable life you're creating for yourself, this tool will be handy. You can highlight your knowledge gaps to decide whether or not you should fill those gaps. The Method helps you pry open those gaps and peek inside.

Becoming Comfortable with Not Knowing

Remember the trap of right and wrong? That's the one where being wrong creates a sneaky feeling that is deviously similar to being right, because we often think we're right when we're not. This trap, plus a lifetime of getting marked down for not knowing, creates an inexperience and discomfort with not knowing. This often results in our grabbing the easy answers and squashing the curiosity necessary to seek the more insightful ones. Identifying *what* you don't know first requires knowing *that* you don't know, giving you more experience and comfort with the feeling. Your reward will be more insightful answers.

Crisping Up Your Goal and Your Message

Once you're more knowledgeable about what you don't know and more comfortable with not knowing, you will be in a better position to let curiosity guide you. You may decide that filling knowledge gaps to achieve one goal will be more fulfilling than filling them to achieve a slightly different goal. Also, replacing justification and fear with curiosity removes the blocks that prevent you from defining and accomplishing your goals. This will help you define your goals more clearly and make achieving them more fulfilling... and more likely.

How to Know What You Don't Know

You are now ready to become strategically curious about what you don't know. Don't feel bad about acknowledging what you don't know, because the results from that acknowledgment will be astonishingly helpful. You'll bust an illusion that we all have about ourselves. Yale researchers Leonid Rozenblit and Frank Keil identified one of the many reasons that we believe we know more than we do when, in fact, our knowledge is superficial at best. They described this as the "illusion of explanatory depth."[15] It's one of our handy mental shortcuts. Our familiarity with things makes us think that we actually know how these things work.

"
To know, is to know that you know nothing. That is the meaning of true knowledge. —SOCRATES

Socrates was right to describe himself as a gadfly, because gadflies sting, and it does sting to know you don't know. Knowing this is also really smart. It may be even smarter to acknowledge it.

Do you assume that not knowing means you can't tackle the problem? Or do you assume that not knowing gives you a better, fresher perspective to tackle the problem? Are you curious about when clichés like "Ignorance is bliss" apply and when they don't?

"
I don't know anything about music. In my line you don't have to. —ELVIS PRESLEY

Not knowing can also create lovely serendipity. The truth is that solutions become more likely when you're open to the fact that you don't already know all the answers.

Exercise 1.1: Get Started

Cha-ching! Give yourself bonus points for acknowledging that you *don't know* how to get started. This exercise will give you a boost.

1. First there's that elevate curiosity hack. Do that.
2. Identify 0 to 3 assumptions you refuse to question or bust. Write them down. For example, if you refuse to bust your assumption in the belief in God or the belief in atheism, write that down.
3. Acknowledge that we are always working with incomplete information. Always.
4. Stand in front of a mirror and specifically describe:
   - How the Cloud works
   - How mortgages turn into secured investment vehicles or other pooled investments
   - How ballots are counted in political elections
   - How energy credits work
   - How pharmaceuticals get to market
   - How bestseller status is calculated
   - How insurance claims affect your life
   - How eyewitness testimony works in a courtroom
   - How the minds of family, friends, or coworkers work
   - Okay, smarty, if you know everything about all of these things, try explaining it all in the Chon nomadic language of Patagonia, Tehuelche.[16]

   Practice talking to the mirror like this from time to time. This will help you break the assumption of knowing and get you comfortable with not knowing.
5. Then say, think, and/or write:
   - I really want to accomplish or be _____, but I am not someone who

knows _____.
- How do I know that I don't know? (For example, do you have someone who helps you reveal the gaps in your knowledge?)

Answer:

- Why do I need to know that I don't know? (For example, do you specifically need to explore a gap in your knowledge to achieve a goal?)

Answer:

❝ *Teach thy tongue to say, "I do not know" and thou shalt progress.* —MAIMONIDES

In addition to the key benefits, some other cool things happen when you poke yourself to question the assumption of knowing:

- You'll see more options (not just choice A or B but perhaps also C, D, E, and/or F).

❝ *I told my dentist my teeth are going yellow. He told me to wear a brown tie.* —RODNEY DANGERFIELD

- Hidden insights will be revealed to you.

❝ *For about a month after my baby was born I bragged to everyone that I had the perfect baby because he never cried. Then I realized those baby monitors have volume control.* —FRANCES DILORINZO

- You'll avoid misjudging based on your limited experience.

> " *I was coming home from kindergarten — well, they told me it was kindergarten. I found out later I had been working in a factory for ten years. It's good for a kid to know how to make gloves.* —ELLEN DEGENERES

- You'll stop yourself from making the same mistakes over and over again.

> " *I wish I had a twin, so I could know what I'd look like without plastic surgery.* —JOAN RIVERS

- Your cognitive biases will be divulged.

> " *Reality is the leading cause of stress amongst those in touch with it.* —LILY TOMLIN

- You'll see things in different ways.

> " *You should always go to other people's funerals; otherwise, they won't come to yours.* —YOGI BERRA

- People will be more likely to help you.

> " *I was walking down Fifth Avenue today, and I found a wallet. I was going to keep it, rather than return it, but I thought: Well, if I lost $150, how would I feel? And I realized I would want to be taught a lesson.*
> —EMO PHILIPS

- You'll reframe situations for better results.

> **❝** *All right, let's not panic. I'll make the money by selling one of my livers. I can get by with one.* —HOMER SIMPSON

- You'll be smarter.

> **❝** *Sometimes the road less traveled is less traveled for a reason.* —JERRY SEINFELD

Every time I adventure out on one of my curiosity quests to meet new people or explore new places, I start by identifying what I don't know—focusing on the stuff that relates to the adventure and the insights I hope to gain.

While preparing for meeting with a prominent witch, I had to acknowledge that I didn't *really* understand the difference between Wicca, Wiccan, witchcraft, witches, warlocks, and pagans. I still don't know whether or not to capitalize some of those words (and I apologize if I did it in a way that does not match your beliefs or preferences). Acknowledging these gaps in my knowledge left me open to surprises and insights that I filled by meeting with a brilliant witch leader, other self-described witches, Wiccans, and pagans, and by attending a Samhain ritual. As it turned out, there was lack of a clear consensus about these differences. One of the many things this made me realize was that, as in all belief systems, no two people believe exactly the same way.

So let's apply this concept of knowing what you don't know to your goal of being remarkable and doing good stuff. Perhaps your mission is to make the world a better place by working to eradicate homelessness in your city, so you decide to channel your work as a member of a board of directors of a homeless charity. How might the process of identifying what you don't know look like?

Addressing problems with homelessness was Sam Ander's beneficial change, and this is a bit of his story.

Do We Always Get What We Deserve?

Sam loved to joke-brag that he traded the last of his red hairs for a black Porsche when he was only thirty-two. A few years before his big Porsche purchase, he had quit college with one year left to join his fraternity brother in a paint start-up that became popular with graffiti artists. His success proved what he had always suspected: hard work results in deserved rewards. Do you agree? Always? Never?

Sam was in a mastermind group of entrepreneurs who drank great scotch and discussed societal problems. One of the biggies was homelessness. He encountered a lot of homeless people in his work, and he decided to do something about it. He wanted to get experience being on a board of directors, so he decided to find and join the board of a high-profile charitable organization working to combat problems of homelessness.

Sam had a lot of assumptions, but he was willing to explore what he did not know. He told me this is what he came up with: "I really want to become a successful contributor to the board and make a difference for homeless people. I am not someone who knows about homelessness, because I've never been homeless. I don't even think I've ever been close to anyone homeless."

Sam delved even deeper into the gaps in his knowledge. With a bit of prodding, he admitted, "I wouldn't know how to live without electricity…at least not for very long. I don't know what gangs run which parts of town. I've never suffered from mental illness, nor have I had a serious brain injury…except that minor concussion from skateboarding in junior high school. I wouldn't know how to use a payday lender or navigate a free medical clinic. I wouldn't know the best places and ways to get free clothing or food. I'm not even sure how the different shelters work."

Several extremely wealthy people were on the board that Sam was hoping to join. He had never been on a board of directors, nor had he ever worked with really wealthy people. Looking back, he told me, "I didn't want to look like a fool. I didn't know how the politics of money and influence played out on a board. As I researched further, I realized that there were a lot of board protocol and legal issues that I did not know."

He delved further and found even more specific knowledge gaps. "I didn't grow up wealthy," he said. "I didn't know the best ways to shelter income from taxes or how to take advantage of tax incentives for low-income development. I didn't know how to strategically contribute to political campaigns, but that was a strategy that other board members understood. I didn't know about the advantages that qualified accredited investors enjoy. I wasn't even sure how to qualify."

As you can probably tell, this stage is where things can get uncomfortable. When there are many things we *do* know, why would we want to think about what we *don't* know? Plus, it's hard to elevate curiosity when it challenges our worldview, but this is where the powerful insights hide.

After identifying and acknowledging what he didn't know, Sam described insights that started to emerge for him.

"I started to understand that the issue of homelessness and how to address it is more complicated than I realized. I was curious to explore whether there is actually an acceptable level of homelessness. Maybe not, but maybe…I was curious about the worst things about homelessness. What are they? Should we have homeless and/or formerly homeless people on the board? Are incentives for the poor (like Section 8 housing) at odds with incentives for wealthier developers (like tax breaks for development)? What's the difference between a handout and a bailout? Are we asking the right questions? It was scary when I made myself seriously consider what specific things would have to occur for me to be homeless. Damn."

I asked Sam whether being strategically curious about identifying what he did not know was helpful for his mission.

"Curiosity was kind of painful because it didn't prop me up. It didn't necessarily confirm what I thought I knew to be true. I used to believe that we all get what we deserve, because I saw my hard work and sacrifice directly result in success. I kind of applied my limited experience to others in a simplistic way. I didn't know that there are so many factors that make these issues more complex. Curiosity challenged my worldview and made it shakier, but ultimately I think I'm more insightful and effective."

The Living Curiously Method does not promise to eradicate homelessness, but the first stage of Step 1 will help you begin to curiously question the assumptions that can hide insights. It helped Sam curiously question assumptions and reveal gaps in his knowledge so that he can now challenge and contribute to the board in important ways.

Now that you have begun to identify gaps in your knowledge, be curious before you're critical...especially of yourself. It can be discouraging to realize how little we know, but it is also liberating because it makes us live more curiously—if we elevate curiosity ahead of self-judgment. You're doing something most people never do in order to experience and accomplish things most people never accomplish. That's remarkable. Cut yourself some slack, give yourself a few more bonus points, and keep going.

Identify What You're Not For

The second stage of Step 1 of the Method involves identifying your *not for*. This includes what you don't stand for and whom your message and mission are not trying to reach. You can call this your nonaudience.

For example, Martin Luther King Jr. did not stand for violent protest. His message of nonviolent protest was not for the followers of Malcolm X's Black Nationalism movement. Of course, the history is more complicated than that, as history always is, but both leaders understood what they did not stand for and whom their message was not for.

Key Benefits

There are three key benefits to identifying what you don't stand for and whom your message and mission is not for:

- Flexing your curiosity muscles
- Creating differentiation
- Understanding your critics (naysayers) and your fans (yay-sayers)

Flexing Your Curiosity Muscles

The less obvious type of self-exploration ("I don't stand for this, and my ideas, products, services, etc., are not for this particular audience") requires curiosity and bravery. Acknowledging what you're not is a lot harder than the more obvious (and less effective) statements like "I'm *all* about this or that!" or "My goal is to help *everyone* on the planet."

Starting with what you're not and identifying your *not for* ignites curiosity because it's more challenging to understand negative language constructions. Negative language constructions use words like *not, no, don't*—just like *what you're not*. You may be good at comprehending negative constructions yourself, but you've probably experienced them not working when you tell your partner or child, "Don't leave your dirty underwear everywhere." Perhaps they just don't hear the "don't" part?

If you find your brain sneaking back to focus on what you *are* all about...wait! You'll have time for that after you curiously consider what you're *not for*. You'll see how much clearer and easier it will be to define what you are once you have defined what you're not.

Creating Differentiation
Identifying what you don't stand for and whom your message is not for are part of creating your personal message, or brand. Believe me, lovely skeptics, I know that the idea of a personal brand can be nauseating and cynicism-inspiring...if you let it. If you have something meaningful to build or work toward, though, it goes beyond ego gratification and popularity. But building your personal brand to achieve your mission must be done and must be done correctly—with heavy doses of strategic curiosity.

Although starting with what you're not sparks deep curiosity resulting in meaningful self-discovery, your mission will most likely involve other people too. This means that there will be some aspect of selling, influencing, persuading, enticing, convincing, cajoling, or arousing. Yuck, you say? You don't do that? Well, unless you want your mission and message to be the best-kept secret, please reconsider.

Because I've always been interested in how sales works, I like the term *arousing the buy curious*. This is selling your idea, or your helpful product or service, in a way that is noble. The goal is for your potential partners, audience, allies, or buyers to begin to ask, "What does it mean? What does it mean for me?" And you can reply, "I'm glad you asked, because you can help me with my mission. This is how I'm changing the world for the better!" Whether they actually buy something or simply buy into your mission, you're using meaningful persuasion to draw them in. Creating differentiation helps do this.

Starting with what you're not and identifying what you are not for elevates the ideas you represent. Similarly, in an argument, conceding a point can elevate the authority of other points of your argument that you don't concede. This is called the blemishing effect, and it's a technique that is powerfully proven in the science of persuasion and influence.[17]

For example, which statement is more persuasive if you're hiring a guide to arrange a travel adventure in Brazil?

> "I am the best one to take you anywhere you want to travel."
> "I'm not the best one to arrange a trip to Europe, *but* I am the best one to arrange your life-changing adventure anywhere in South America."

What if you're hiring a consultant for your business to help you achieve location independence?

> "This will work for all your business needs."
> "My consulting services are not optimized for businesses without an online presence, *but* I can help you stop renting your time if you are open to expanding your program online."

What about when you're ordering at a new restaurant?

> "Everything on our menu is great!"
> "The chef is not an expert in Russian cooking, so our borscht is just okay, *but* she just returned from Spain and the tapas will transform your life."

Acknowledging a weakness before the strength provides proper focus on the strength. According to Robert Cialdini, the king of persuasion science, the word *but* sets aside the information that was received and focuses attention on the next thing. What you're not is not necessarily a weakness, but starting with what you're not properly directs the focus to exactly what you are when you get to that next.

Understanding Your Critics (Naysayers) and Your Fans (Yaysayers)
Do you have a way to weed out worthless haters from constructive critics? Identifying what you don't stand for and whom your message is not for helps you laser-focus on your target audience from the very beginning. It also helps you field feedback later when your good stuff project is in process or is finished.

Someone who is not perfect for the remarkable life you're creating is not a hater for feeling that way. Nor is he necessarily a hater for letting you know he feels that way. He may just be strategically wrong for your message.

For example, my first book, *Arousing the Buy Curious*,[12] was not written for people easily offended by language. It is not filtered for a super-conservative work environment or for highly sensitive, conservative folk. Although the book is chock-full of general sales techniques and true and hilarious stories, it is not for people with zero interest in ever buying or selling real estate. Starting with what I am not provided the self-discovery necessary for me to know this and helped me evaluate what I should do with the feedback I received.

One ultra-conservative guy wrote to tell me that I was the reason for everything wrong with the world. While I thought that was a slight exaggeration, it was also true that he had zero interest or experience in real estate beyond thinking it was a sleazy profession. Whether he was just a hater or not was irrelevant, because he was a naysayer that fell smack within what I am not—he was strategically wrong for my message. It was liberating to see that I could ignore him and his judgment.

One jovial woman sent me a rather hilarious email about how much she loved *Arousing the Buy Curious* for the funny stories, but she had zero interest in anything relating to real estate or sales. When she offered that I should write another book of funny stories, I appreciated her positive feedback and graciously thanked her, but I took no further action. She was a yaysayer who also fell within the category for whom I'm not.

Another woman was an owner of a large real estate company, and she had a wicked sense of humor and loved the psychology of sales and persuasion. However, she was very critical of the naughty language because she felt it prevented broader distribution of the book within her company. I analyzed her naysaying because she *was* my perfect target audience—she did *not* fall within the category of what I am not. Eventually I heeded her advice and launched the safe-for-work edition of *Arousing the Buy Curious* (which, strangely enough, elevated sales of the raw, unfiltered edition).

I got great feedback from edgier folk for whom real estate was their job or hobby. These yaysayers fell directly in the target market for *Arousing the Buy Curious*, and it was and still is important to maintain what resonates for them when I speak and write about *Arousing the Buy Curious*.

There will always be people who love to cause trouble by being more critical and threatening than our activities, creations, ideas, products, and visions warrant. The invisibility cloak of the virtual world is often mistaken for invincibility, so many dish out the negative crap in a way that they never would if they had to address you face-to-face. It's good to be curious enough to differentiate between a threat and valuable feedback. Curiosity prevents mislabeling your audience and losing valuable information in the process. This process will allow you to focus your valuable time and attention on analyzing the feedback from the people who align with what you are for.

> **"** *I'm sure there's somebody out there who doesn't like Betty White because she's short and has white hair.*
> —ELLEN DEGENERES

The truth is that the exact thing that makes people love you is often the exact same thing that makes other people hate you. The bigger you put yourself out there, the more you will be revered...and reviled.

> **"** *First they ignore you, then they laugh at you, then they fight you, then you win.* —MAHATMA GANDHI

Just like I did with the feedback on *Arousing the Buy Curious,* as you progress with your mission, it's helpful to remember whom your mission is not for so you know what to do with the feedback you'll receive:

- If rejection (naysayers) of you, your ideas, or your products comes from the zone of your nonaudience, it doesn't warrant consideration. You're not trying to reach this audience. Ignore.
- If rejection (different naysayers) of you, your ideas, or your products comes from the zone of your target audience, you know to address challenges in your messaging or products. Analyze.

- If acceptance (yaysayers) comes from the zone of your nonaudience, these niceties could misdirect you down a path of time-sinking projects outside of your mission. This too is an audience you're not optimizing to reach. Appreciate.
- If acceptance (different yaysayers) comes from the zone of your target audience, you are on target with your idea's messaging. Maintain.

While you're identifying feedback based on these four categories, be sure you constantly elevate curiosity. You'll gain powerful insights while also taking the sting out of the feedback.

Coffee snobs regularly poke fun at Dutch Bros. Coffee's crazy beverage names like Annihilator, Kahlua Kicker, Cocomo, The Cure, Double Torture, ER 911 (384 mg of caffeine), and Blue Rebel Energy Drink, but this company clearly knows what they're not about and who they're not for. Here is their story.

Can You Create a Coffee Counterculture without Counters?

Perhaps most people would consider this story one of amazing business success. But when I talked with Travis Boersma, it became clear that he would more accurately describe the story of Dutch Bros. Coffee as one of life success. It's a story still being told.

In spite of being seventeen years apart, brothers Dane and Travis Boersma were extremely close. As their family dairy farm struggled in the 1980s and early 1990s, their dream of becoming the third generation to run the family farm became increasingly unrealistic. Travis was curious about exploring a business that they could do together, and he suggested that they start a coffee cart to sell espresso. Like many people in early 1990, Dane was unfamiliar with espresso. He was, however, an experienced entrepreneur, having owned Dairy Queen franchises in his early twenties.

Travis described the experience: "I had the great fortune of having a brother that was seventeen years older than me. My curiosity, drive, and willingness to take risks combined with his ability to be stable and wise. He wanted to overdeliver on the experience long before that was something many people talked about. He had been in the service business and had awareness of being present. He knew the value of listening and having great conversation. He was clear on what's important...and what's not."

By the time the brothers launched their first coffee cart in 1992, froofy espresso drinks were a national craze. Starbucks was leading the charge with 140 outlets, revenue of $73.5 million, and an announcement that they were going public.

Dutch Bros. started out—and remains, through tremendous growth today—decidedly and strategically unlike Starbucks or any other coffee place. Dutch Bros. Coffee broke the paradigm of a coffee shop being a quiet place to sit down and relax at a table or to mingle at a coffee counter. The vast majority of Dutch Bros. Coffee outlets are drive-throughs with a buzz-speed experience not unlike the buzz one gets by consuming their highly caffeinated beverages. Tragically, Dane Boersma died of ALS in 2009, but the company has remained true to the vision Dane shared with his bro, Travis.

Dutch Bros. Coffee is *not*: tame, uniform, quiet, old-school retro, run by older folk, serious, necessarily about great coffee, reminiscent of elegant European coffee shops, a place to conduct business, dive-y, a place for contemplation, a place to read a good book, snarky or angsty, publicly traded, leisurely, afraid of getting wet, about charging luxury prices, for hiding the power and addictive pleasure of caffeine, above brewing under a rotating disco ball, or too cool for life-affirming inspiration. While coffee drinks at other companies are made and served by baristas, Dutch Bros. Coffee's is made and served by "broistas."

Talking with Travis confirmed everything I had experienced and read about Dutch Bros. "The culture is so vital to what we do. It's often described as love, trust, character, wisdom, and integrity. We describe it as don't be a 'D.' Don't be detrimental, discouraging, a dick. It's not your conventional company. It's more about having a positive outlook and living by the optimist creed. It's doing the right thing."

Some cringe at the broistas' constantly cheerful language.

❝ *Epic, bro! You crush it! We're all jacked on caffeine, dude. Awesome!* —Dutch Bros. broista

Dutch Bros. doesn't serve coffee any differently than they would serve beer at a kegger. Bro, they're hosting a party to celebrate life. That's the differentiator.

Dutch Bros. is not for Wall Street or IPO-hungry investors, and they allow franchise opportunities for only their best and most trusted employees.

"We want to find a compelling future for employees, and to ask and figure out how we build this company [so it] has a culture that is sustainable for generations beyond...for my kids' kids' kids."

Travis and the company are clear about what they are not and equally clear about what they are. The Dutch Creed[18] clearly defines the company and its employees as "being positive and lovin' life." The nipple-topped coffee lid embossed with "We'll get through this together" and the Dutch Mafia swag clearly reflect their unique cult-of-coffee culture.

As Travis explained, curiosity is a driving force for the company. "I think curiosity is something that has always been a part of my being, my makeup. I'm fascinated with human behavior. The curiosity of what's possible. Where can we go?"

Dan Buck, VP of marketing at Dutch Bros., added, "The moment you stop being curious and stop asking questions is the moment you stop growing. We feed ourselves with a constant swirl of questions. I fear the day that we come in here and we have no more questions to ask."

Artisanal coffee aficionados may snicker, but the growth of Dutch Bros. is no laughing matter. They have turned the business of selling an addictive liquid into a positive partying force and, in so doing, have become the largest privately held drive-through coffee chain in North America.[19]

Travis summed it up with, "We have a giant army of customers, and we're going to war for love."

Exercise 1.2: Get to Know Yourself

This exercise includes a series of identifying statements. Do some of it or do all of it. The key is that these statements will get you started identifying stuff you may not know and stuff you may not stand for. All knowledge is relative, and answering these questions will provoke a curious way of thinking. Elevate curiosity waaaay ahead of any smidgeon of shame, embarrassment, or self-criticism. Pour yourself a beverage of your choice and have fun.

Grab something to write on, or write in your book. Folks, please don't write on your ebook. Go through the list and write the letter(s) to complete each statement. You may not have ever considered many of the following statements or maybe they are all you think about. Either way, it is okay to take extra time to research some or all if you want to learn more before answering. It's like an open-book and open-mind quiz.

After you go through the Method, you may want to share this exercise with a friend or revisit it as a great way to see your progress. Relax in knowing that it's impossible for you not to get an A or a high B+ on this exercise.

1. I am not a believer in:
   a. Ghosts
   b. Evolution
   c. Powerful people
   d. Fate

2. I am not knowledgeable about:
   a. Technology
   b. The entertainment industry
   c. Globalization
   d. Ecology

3. I am not understanding of:
   a. Greedy people
   b. Lazy people

   c. Brilliant people
   d. Addicted people

4. I am not:
   a. Urban
   b. Suburban
   c. Rural
   d. Foreign

5. I am not knowledgeable about:
   a. Generational poverty
   b. Debt structuring
   c. Immigration policy
   d. Inherited wealth

6. I am not one who knows about:
   a. Mental competitions
   b. Surviving in the wild
   c. Cultural differences in morality
   d. High-stakes gambling

7. I am not:
   a. Powerful
   b. Spiritual
   c. Flexible
   d. Healthy

8. I am not:
   a. Sensual
   b. Experimental
   c. Confident
   d. Street smart

9. I am not knowledgeable about:
   a. Farming
   b. Real estate

    c. Banking

    d. Programming

10. I am not:
    a. A party lover
    b. A good writer
    c. A victim
    d. A rule breaker

11. I am not a lover of:
    a. Animals
    b. Fashion
    c. Fancy cars
    d. Exotic foods

12. I am not:
    a. A believer
    b. A skeptic
    c. Funny
    d. Scientific

13. I am not:
    a. Psychic
    b. Traditional
    c. Motivational
    d. Contrarian

14. I am not knowledgeable about:
    a. Racial profiling
    b. Sex discrimination
    c. Military lifestyle
    d. Life behind bars

15. I am not:
    a. Technical
    b. Mechanical

c. Musical
d. Athletic

Are you elevating curiosity?

16. I am not:
    a. Politically correct
    b. Romantic
    c. A fantasizer
    d. Controlling

17. I am not:
    a. Tough
    b. White
    c. Earthy
    d. Worldly

18. I am not:
    a. Social
    b. Quiet
    c. Private
    d. Quick

19. I am not:
    a. Liberal
    b. Convincing
    c. Clever
    d. Dangerous

20. I am not knowledgeable about:
    a. Pop culture
    b. History
    c. Politics
    d. Art

20. I am not:
    e. A planner
    f. An instigator
    g. A big company person
    h. A dreamer

21. I am not:
    a. A world traveler
    b. A camper
    c. An inventor
    d. An attention seeker

22. I am not knowledgeable about:
    a. Medicine
    b. Anthropology
    c. Linguistics
    d. Psychology

23. I am not:
    a. A good dancer
    b. A slow learner
    c. A swearer
    d. Sexually brave

24. I am not:
    a. Agreeable
    b. Serious
    c. Observant
    d. Normal

25. I am not experienced with:
    a. Mental illness
    b. Language barriers
    c. Physical limitations
    d. Refugees

26. I am not:
    a. A monotheist
    b. Wrong
    c. An atheist
    d. Worried

27. I am not:
    a. Responsible
    b. Open-minded
    c. Honest
    d. Deserving

28. I am not knowledgeable about:
    a. Parenting
    b. Cosmetics
    c. Self-employment
    d. Drugs

Add your own list to the worksheet (or in your steel-trap memory if you're cheating a bit by doing this as a thought experiment). For example, if you're focusing on helping the world understand gender issues, it may (or may not) be useful to add:

I am not:
    e. Female
    f. Chromosomally strictly female
    g. Traditionally or cis male
    h. Male

Add your own:

I am not:

Nor am I:

How'd you do? Are you more curious about yourself?

Before you move on to the next exercise, which is really an extension of this exercise, promise yourself an astonishing amount of fun and insight regardless of whether you ever get a crisp definition of yourself. Give yourself a bonus point or two if you understand the limitless power of never committing to a totally crisp definition of yourself.

" *Too often we…enjoy the comfort of opinion without the discomfort of thought.* —JOHN F. KENNEDY

Although it might be easier to stop now and receive an assessment that you are an I.E.O.P.D. personality type, or your passion aligns with other Maestro archetypes, or your horcrux is a platypus, this exercise won't do that—curiosity isn't that tidy. Also, beware of that pesky Forer effect,[20] which is a bias that makes us believe our own personality assessments and horoscopes.This type of untidier exercise will lubricate your mind for curiosity and will help you tap your *own* curiosity to create your *own* insights. See? Remarkable.

" *Don't be intimidated by what you don't know. That can be your greatest strength and ensure that you do things differently from everyone else.*
—SARA BLAKELY, FOUNDER OF SPANX

Exercise 1.3: Fill In the Gaps
Now that we've explored what you're not, it's time to take a look at your knowledge gaps. Acknowledging gaps in your knowledge does not require you to fill them all. Your strategy is to become aware of the gaps so that what you're *not* going to do becomes as important as what you *are* going to do. Use the answers from the previous exercise here, or add more ideas from your beautiful, gap-filled brain.

Propulsion

1. List 3 things that you do not know that you will now be more curious about.
2. List 3 things that you do not know that you must be more curious about to effectively accomplish your beneficial change. These can be the same as or different than the things you listed for number 1.
3. Follow your curiosity to explore adding knowledge to the information gaps that most relate to your beneficial change. The beauty is that the gaps will never be full—you can keep filling forever if you want to, or never start. But if you're not willing to take the time to add knowledge to those gaps, ask yourself how the depth of the gaps affects your ability to tackle your mission. It may or may not matter, but it's important to be curious about it.

For example, when I first did this exercise, I wanted to be more curious about the different ways rural and urban Americans establish our political differences. That was on my list for #1. Since understanding this subject could very well be an important part of the beneficial change I'm trying to create and inspire, this was also on my list for #2. Because I'm an urban Northwesterner, to do #3, I headed to the Louisiana bayou.

I expected to meet and chat with the fascinating swamp tour guide whose family had lived on the bayou for generations. Meeting his sister, Meg, was an added bonus, in no small part because we were nearly opposites. Meg's babies swam in the bayou with sharp-toothed 'gators; mine played soccer in the park with fuzzy-tailed squirrels. Although I had lived in the Deep South right after grad school, I was neither knowledgeable about nor experienced with Southern rural life. Meg's understanding of the importance or unimportance of various government services was fascinatingly different from my own. Living off the land that had been in her Cajun family for generations had created a kind of self-sufficiency that was different from mine. She and her kids catch, prepare, and eat creatures of the swamp; understand the importance of the bayou as a protector to inland areas; and take an active role in its preservation. I've caught about four fish and three crawdads in my life, and I was as distantly indignant about the government's neglect of the levees leading up to the devastation of Hurricane Katrina as I was about the stubbornness of folks who continue to live below sea level.

I learned that this rural, self-sufficient lifestyle makes a significant positive impact on greater society. Meg doesn't feel the need for government to dictate and regulate what trees to preserve and what creatures to extract from the swamp that is her front yard—she and her neighbors already know that protecting those resources is a vital part of everyday life on the bayou. This is vastly different from the perception of many city folk who want manicured parks and bike paths from government. Political divides are certainly more complex than this, but perhaps this hints at one of the reasons for the political divide between urban and rural Americans. Elevating curiosity and strategically using curiosity to fill in some of my knowledge gaps has made me more understanding and appreciative of the significant differences between rural and urban voters.

" *It ain't what you don't know that gets you into trouble. It's what you know for sure that just ain't so.* —MARK TWAIN

4. Next, since we don't give ourselves enough time to stop doing...
   - Think.
   - Breathe through your nose (or STFU).
   - Be curious.
5. Rescan at least 7 of the identifying statements from Exercise 1.2 while asking yourself: What does this mean? What does this mean for me? Feel free to briefly squint your eyes for maximum concentration.
6. Are you ready to embrace what you do not stand for? There is no right answer, but now it's time to take a shot at answering:

> *I don't stand for_____.*
>
> Do you want to keep what you don't stand for, or are you inspired to change?
>
> 7. Identify who you're not trying to reach (your non-audience).
>
> *My message is not for _____.*

Here's what I included when I started with what I'm not and defined my nonaudience:

The Living Curiously Method is ill suited for people who want to live in worlds with no shades of gray—those who want to continue to only value evidence that supports their worldview and to reject evidence to the contrary. I'll take a bolder and more controversial position and suggest that the Method is not for the millions of people who love and adhere to *The Secret*, for example. That does not mean that those who enjoy and follow the philosophy of *The Secret* cannot find value in the Method; it is just not designed with that audience in mind.

" *All we all have to decide is what to do with the time that is given us.* —J. R. R. TOLKIEN

Bonus Round*
If you feel like overachieving and diving deeper into curiosity with this exercise, check out Part IV, Exercise 6.5.

Hopefully, this first step of the Method has ignited your curiosity and made you more comfortable with what you don't know. Now you have the tools to acknowledge sacred assumptions and bust limiting ones. By now you realize that your strategy for accomplishing your beneficial change starts with what you're not, what you're not going to do, and who you're not trying to inspire. You have done the harder internal work, and now it is time for a bit more fun. Put on your gloves because we're going dumpster-diving, and it's bound to get messy.

> " *Every new beginning comes from some other beginning's end.* — ATTRIBUTED TO LUCIUS SENECA (AND THE NINETIES ROCK BAND SEMISONIC)

And so you've begun.

Step 2: Dumpster-Dive Your Life

" *My life is my message.* —Mahatma Gandhi

Now that you know a bit about what you're not, it is time to get curious about what defines you. This will reveal what makes you uniquely remarkable. We all have public, private, and secret lives, but we often don't pay attention to them all. The most useful, authentic, and defining tidbits about you often hide in the dumpster of your life. What conversations, stories, and artifacts have you tossed away? What's in your life's dumpster that will help you connect with others in profound ways to inspire and accomplish beneficial change?

There are two key things to do as you're diving through the dumpster of your life:

- Excavate early conversations
- Excavate early experiences

Although unearthing early conversations and early experiences from our life's dumpster is incredibly valuable, many things stop us from diving inside. Here are just a few possibilities:

70

- We're scared of what we may find and remember.
- We're ashamed of what we tossed away.
- We discount the contents of our life's dumpster as unimpressive or mundane.
- Our belief that the best is yet to come devalues the lessons of what we left behind.
- We forget that the astonishing way we relate to others is often with the messiest stories…the exact stories we find in the dumpster of our lives.
- Our fear of getting messy overpowers curiosity about what we will find.

Curiosity is bravery's kissing cousin. These cousins will help you overcome the fear of getting too messy when you dive into your life's dumpster. It will be worth it. The unique stories you dig out hold the keys to your remarkability. The benefits of diving far outweigh the dangers.

Key Benefits

There are three key benefits to dumpster-diving your life:

- Uncovering signature stories that are authentic and unique
- Providing connection with and inspiration for others
- Extracting valuable forgotten lessons

Uncovering Signature Stories that Are Authentic and Unique

To do good stuff in this noisy world, it is critical to crank up the signal of your personal signature stories. The more that your stories can only be told about you, the louder and clearer your message will resonate. Many people can talk about degrees they've earned, honors they've been awarded, and companies they've built, and those often impressively establish authority. However, the stories your friends and family members tell about you, and the early conversations and experiences you excavate from the dumpster of your life, help you differentiate yourself in more engaging and authentic ways. When later you combine the excavations of your dumpster stories with your authority-enhancing honors, awards, and accomplishments, your unique personal brand emerges. And then it's so much easier to inspire beneficial change.

❝ *Few people even scratch the surface, much less exhaust the contemplation of their own experience.*
—RANDOLPH BOURNE, ESSAYIST

Providing Connection with and Inspiration for Others

Deep within your life's dumpster is a lot of real, differentiating, and unique content, but this does not change the fact that we all have our share of messiness. Go ahead and get dirty, because this messiness is where we all connect. How often are you inspired by people who have overcome messiness to accomplish remarkable things? You will inspire others in the same way. The fact that you moved beyond your messiness will provide inspiration and a road map for others to do the same.

Extracting Valuable Forgotten Lessons

The third benefit of dumpster-diving your life is extracting valuable forgotten lessons. Lessons from your past provide clues for uncovering who you are and why. What made you think the way you think? What made you love who you love? What made you question what so many others in the world believe without question? What created your opinions? When did you learn that? How do you know that? What contributed to your remarkability? What else can dumpster-diving your life help you remember?

❝ *Life can only be understood backwards; but it must be lived forwards.* —SØREN KIERKEGAARD

The following exercises will guide you through dumpster-diving your life.

Exercise 2.1: Prepare to Dumpster-Dive

Dumpster-diving is one of those tasks that work best when you do some preparation beforehand. This exercise will walk you through that.

1. Identify 3 people who knew you before you accomplished anything that is included on your resume. List them now and answer the following questions from their perspectives:
   - What would they say that you gravitated toward?
   - What would they say that you were naturally good at?
   - What would they say that you loved to do?
   - What metaphor would they use to describe you?
   - How would they bedazzle your resume?
2. If you have an opportunity, actually ask your 3 people the same 5 questions. How are their responses similar to what you thought? How are they different?
3. Think of someone you know personally whose life you admire. Think of another person you have never met whom you also admire. Why do you admire these people? What moment did you first realize you admire these people?

Lubrication

> **❝***I blame my mother for my poor sex life. All she told me was 'the man goes on the top and the woman underneath.' For three years my husband and I slept in bunk beds.* —JOAN RIVERS

Dumpster-diving our lives is critical preparation for all of the remaining steps of the Living Curiously Method. It helps us to understand ourselves so we can connect with others to inspire and create beneficial change.

Larry Chusid is an unconventional thinker and animal lover who creates and inspires beneficial change in the world.

Dumpster-diving his life has provided the lessons and context for all that he does. Here is his story.

Can We Cure Diabetes by Giving Away Healthy Pet Food?

Over seven million pet meals have been served at the pet food bank since the large man with wheezing breath shuffled through the first, leaky warehouse, but Larry still remembers him. In addition to being one of his earliest customers, the struggling man was memorable because of his unusual request—a half order of dog food.

Larry explained, "I was sweeping the floor when he approached me the first time with his unusual request. I knew it was just as easy to prepare a full order [of dog food] for the man to take back to his dog, but the man specifically wanted half an order because his dog was, as the man described, 'fat, lazy, and old.' I gave him a half an order. The man consistently came back requesting and receiving just a half an order of dog food."

You'll see why I wanted to chat with Larry. However, when I first explained the Living Curiously project to him, he was quite a bit more skeptical than most. He peppered me with questions about living curiously and then claimed that he was not particularly curious. I suspected otherwise.

When we finally connected, Larry started with sharing what he is not. He didn't use that specific language, but I hadn't shared anything about the Method in advance. He claimed not to know much about technology. It was as clear that he does not stand for self-aggrandizement. as it was clear that his mission is not optimized for non–pet people. Step 1 of the Method. Check. He then went on to explain that he has always been a problem solver, and then, without prompting, he shared these stories from the dumpster of his life.

Larry explained how, as a young adult, he would scour the streets after dark, looking for homeless people to help. On the streets he saw a lot of sacred human-pet relationships. He related to these relationships, and he understood why impoverished, hungry people would share what little food they had with their cherished pets. He told me that often pets are the only family people have and that the food they share with their pets is often the only thing keeping the pets out of shelters…until it's just not enough.

Larry related a cycle that goes like this: "Impoverished people share their scarce human food with their pets, and go hungry [themselves]. Human food is not optimized for pets, so pets become increasingly unhealthy. The unhealthier pets become harder and more expensive to care for. Unhealthy pets lead to unhealthy people, as more and more food and resources are sacrificed to care for the less healthy pet. Ultimately, the only option is to give up the pet. I saw how this frequently led to depression...and worse."

That early experience from the dumpster of Larry's life plays a huge role in his personal story. So did this earlier one: "I don't know if I was six or seven, but my mom always told the story of how I hopped home from school on one frosty, winter day, having given one of my boots to a less fortunate friend. I guess I am curious, because I have always liked to look for and find practical solutions to seemingly bigger problems."

Years later, Larry applied that same sensible problem-solving approach that his mother described to the issue of hungry people and hungry pets. He explained it to me with, "Many foundations and organizations, whose mission it is to feed, care for, and solve problems of the homeless, believe that the focus should be on people, not animals. Charities that do focus on providing food for pets channel their donations to shelters. Ironically, this scarce pet food is potentially the very food that would keep a large number of pets out of shelters in the first place," Larry emphasized. "No-kill shelters accept fewer pets, as they must be selective, given limited space to keep animals for an unlimited time. Regular animal shelters are forced to euthanize unclaimed animals. Unhealthy pets usually suffer a predictable fate."

Larry's curious questions were: What are we doing wrong? Is there a different way to solve the problem of hungry people and their hungry pets? Are we solving the right problem? What if we could actually tackle the problem of feeding hungry people by feeding their hungry pets?

After spending many years working with homeless and impoverished folks and developing these curious questions, Larry started the Pongo Fund and the Pongo Fund Pet Food Bank. The food bank is a full-time, volunteer-driven distribution network fighting animal hunger by providing emergency healthy pet food assistance to anyone in honest need. Because of the Pongo Fund, thousands of families have remained intact and thousands of pets have avoided shelters.

A year after first encountering the large man with the strange request, Larry was sweeping the floor of the warehouse; he loves to sweep. He noticed that an unfamiliar man kept staring at him. Finally the man caught Larry's eye.

"Do you recognize me?"

"No, should I?"

The man explained that he was the man that used to come in for half an order of dog food. The healthy-looking man went on to explain that once his dog started eating the nutritious food from the Pongo Fund Pet Food Bank, he started to have more energy and demanded to be walked. This forced the man out of the house on long walks. The man and his dog both started losing weight. Pretty soon, the man had lost so much weight that his doctor told him that he was no longer diabetic. Meanwhile, his dog was back to a full, healthy diet. Healthy pet food had saved both of their lives.

These conversations and experiences from the dumpster of Larry's life not only help Larry better understand himself and remember the lessons from his past, but they also help him connect with and inspire others to volunteer and donate. Without these others, as Larry is quick to point out, the Pongo Fund would not exist.

So how can you reignite curiosity in your own stories that you have tossed in the dumpster of your life?

❝
As a child, I was more afraid of tetanus shots than, for example, Dracula. —DAVE BARRY

Exercise 2.2: Get Messy

Reflection

Our past is full of so many conversations. The simple fact that you remember a particular one means that it is of some significance…at least enough that your memory saved it in a retrievable location. But often the most authentic conversations are not the ones that we have infused with significance, but rather, they are mundane conversations that we have discarded in our life's dumpster. These may require triggers to access, and this is exactly what this exercise provides—triggers.

Elevate curiosity and...dumpster-dive your life for early conversations by completing these statements:

1. When I was about eight years old, I remember my _____ speaking with me about _____.

2. In my family we never spoke about _____, but I always wondered.

3. In other families I imagine they never talked about _____ as much as we did.

4. I was told that I was_____ and that was a _____ thing.

5. When I asked about_____, I'll never forget what _____ told me.

6. If I hadn't been told _____, I would have never _____.

7. One thing we spoke about in private that we would never speak about in public was _____.

8. The conversation that taught me the most was the one I had with _____ about _____.

9. Other families were so different from mine because I assume they talked about _____, and that's just not something we ever did.

10. I wasn't forbidden to talk about _____, but I got the impression that I shouldn't or _____ might happen.

Then draw a picture of the one person who you feel had the smallest big impact on your life. Done.

❝ *When you look closely at anything familiar, it kind of transmogrifies into something unfamiliar.*
—ALEXANDRA HOROWITZ, COGNITIVE SCIENTIST

Remember to remember. Memories of conversations trigger memories of experiences; memories of experiences trigger memories of conversations. Triggering memories of both conversations and experiences sparks more memories. This will give you the greatest chance of finding the most differentiating kernels of your glorious self.

Because memories are constructs of our sneaky human brains, the exact same conversation or the exact same experience can create distinctly different memories for different people at different times and in different contexts.[21] Although this exercise is for you, feel free to discuss it with other folks hanging around your life's dumpster. You'll witness how strange and different our memories can be— even memories of the exact same conversations and experiences.

❝ *Childhood is like being drunk. Everyone remembers what you said and did except you.* —UNKNOWN

Reflection

Exercise 2.3: Get Messier
Elevate curiosity and...dumpster-dive your life for early experiences by completing these statements:

1. When I was about nine years old, I remember going to _____ with my _____.
2. Every year my _____ went to _____, except the one time when I remember we _____.
3. When I first _____, I knew that I would be _____.
4. My earliest memory of _____ is so inconsistent with what I believe about _____.

5. If I hadn't experienced _____, I would never believe _____.

6. What I think or feel about my _____ had nothing to do with my experience of _____.

7. Other people never experienced _____ the way I did.

8. I know I'm right about _____ because of my experience of _____.

9. The specific experience of _____ is one that uniquely defines my brand of _____.

10. I thought I knew it all until I experienced _____.

11. My first major disappointment was _____.

12. The first time I remember thinking, *I don't want to end up like him/her,* was _____.

Now draw your childhood bedroom.

Exercise 2.4: Put It All Together

If you want to marinate on the first three exercises before forging ahead, that's totally fine. Take your time, because it's important to not get so overwhelmed with swarming ideas that you get stifled.

Propulsion

1. When you're ready, use these early conversations and early experiences to generate least 3 personal and sharable stories. Any 3 stories will do for now.

2. Think about how each story could potentially have relevance to your mission, idea, book, product—to the good stuff you want to do.

3. Now, look over your resume, internet dating profiles, website, blog, and/or social media persona and identify the accomplishments, titles, and/or roles that provide you with your authority.

> 4. Link the 3 stories you extracted from this dumpster-diving experience with the key titles or roles of authority. Start to see how your signature story begins to emerge.

Here's an example of linking dumpster-diving stories. I promised to call this person Marv.

When Marv was eight years old, he was terrified by a costumed aardvark at a theme park, but he felt embarrassed by being a little too old to be afraid of a person in a costume. Like all of the characters at the theme park, the costumed aardvark was under strict orders to never break character. However, the aardvark could see that Marv was scared, so he risked his job by removing his costume in public while calmingly showing Marv the inside of the costume and the mechanics of how the blinking eyes worked.

Did you dig up any simple stories like this? This was one of Marv's stories, but he wasn't sure of the relevance. He just remembered that he was so grateful for the guy who not only risked his job by taking off the aardvark costume but also helped him save face by showing him the inner workings of the costume. It took focused curiosity to determine how this silly story might be relevant. It allowed Marv to realize that this theme park event was when he first learned to question rules when the consequences of blindly following them could be less effective or even harmful.

Marv's realization turned out to be highly relevant because this lesson has been a guiding force in his life. He realized that this lesson led him to question rules in college when he created a whole new curriculum for himself...without permission. The college rules originally said that he couldn't step outside prescribed curricular options, but the rules were later amended after Marv's persistence. When the college later adopted his curriculum, the award he won was a big factor in his graduate school scholarship.

What lesson can you tie to something you found in your life's dumpster? It doesn't have to be angsty or deep. How can you link that to the good stuff you want to do?

Recently, Marv has created an amazing coaching process. Learning how to safely question rules is a big part of his process. There are a lot of coaches, and it has been a challenge to explain why his process is as amazing and as different as it is. He has been working on how to integrate his signature story and is now considering calling it the Aardvark Process.

The story of the costumed aardvark is silly, but it's an example of how the tidbits hiding in your life's dumpster provide hints and lessons that can apply in completely unforeseen ways.

> 5. How could you redo your brand, key personal stories, or one signature story based on this exercise? How could your redo your resume? How will this help you do good stuff?

"*The past is never dead. It's not even past.*
—WILLIAM FAULKNER

What we find in the dumpsters of our lives provides key ingredients in our recipe for connecting with others. Just as we need to understand the ingredients in the foods we eat in order to understand what makes us unhealthy, we need to understand where we come from to understand ourselves...*and* how we relate to others.

Although early conversations and early experiences provide critical ingredients for our signature stories, our dumpster is constantly being filled with new contents that we mistakenly discount as useless debris. Keep your dumpster close by for regular diving to find new ways to connect with different audiences. It will make your life more adventurous.

The process of delving into what makes us who we are takes time, skill, and bravery. It will establish how you want to be known in the world, which will be powerfully helpful in creating beneficial change and inspiring others to do so too. You just have to be curious enough to get a little messy. Follow your curiosity.

You are now ready to move from the first two curious-about-yourself steps of the Living Curiously Method to the next two curious-about-others steps. Give yourself three to six bonus points for your good progress.

> **"***If you can't get rid of the skeleton in your closet, you'd best teach it to dance.* —George Bernard Shaw

Step 3: Cross-Pollinate

> **"** *Cross-pollinators can create something new and better through the unexpected juxtaposition of seemingly unrelated ideas or concepts. They often innovate by discovering a clever solution in one context or industry, then translating it successfully to another.*
> —TOM KELLEY, AUTHOR OF *THE TEN FACES OF INNOVATION*

The next two steps of the Living Curiously Method help you focus your curiosity outward.

Cross-pollinating is mixing thoughts, ideas, insights, questions, answers, and approaches of people from different backgrounds, interests, experiences, knowledge, and industries. It is enhanced by exposure to and experience in different places. Cross-pollinating is adventurous, but it requires curiosity to reap the biggest benefits.

Cross-pollinating will expand your networks, help you get and share ideas, expose you to new viewpoints, and provide opportunities to influence others to join you in doing good stuff. It will also help you generate and evaluate many potential right answers. This is critical because doing good stuff very rarely results from limiting yourself to your own one right answer...even when it seems that way.

In general, the idea of cross-pollination makes intuitive sense. Add the ingredients of different people; mix in a variety of places, adventures, and ideas; and—poof!—creativity, innovation, and insights spew from the cauldron of cross-pollination. With the added spice of curiosity, this is probably closer to the truth of where good ideas really come from than the claim that one person had a eureka moment out of nowhere. Great ideas may seem like they come out of nowhere, but do they? Getting curiouser.

Let's face it. We all share a natural tendency to gravitate toward people and places that are familiar and similar. Even adventurous souls like us need to be reminded to actively break away from the familiar and similar. The way out of this rut is to purposefully:

- Collide with fear-inducing people and places
- Collide with intrigue-inducing people and places

That's all it takes to cross-pollinate!

A lot of my curiosity questing and adventures have been collision courses in cross-pollination. One week I hung out with top behavior researchers, a gun shop owner, and a guy who shared lessons learned from living in an abandoned railroad car. I have rarely had special access to certain types of people because of a fancy job title or impressive family connections, but it's great if you do. Most of the time, I simply called and emailed people that I wanted to meet and told them I was working on living curiously or testing this Method for *Living Curiously*. Other times I just showed up and explained it in person. As the project became a wee bit more public, I started to have people contact me who were interested in sharing the role of curiosity in their lives. My point is, the opportunities for cross-pollinating are always available to you—just ask and explain that you're working on living curiously. The three magic words that will help curious questions not be viewed as judgmental questions are: *Out. Of. Curiosity.* Just ask.

> **"** *If you think it's hard to meet new people, try picking up the wrong golf ball.* —JACK LEMMON

Cross-pollinating is officially the third step in the Living Curiously Method. If you take the time to go through this detailed process, chances are good that cross-pollinating will become an enriching and adventurous part of your life. Even if you only have time to try bits and pieces of this step, it will expand your mind so you can reap some of the cool benefits of cross-pollinating. You'll miss a little if you cheat a little, but I won't tell.

Key Benefits

There are three key benefits to cross-pollinating:

- Fueling innovation and generating new ideas
- Enhancing your adventures with insights
- Getting smarter

Fueling Innovation and Generating New Ideas

Research shows that cross-pollination results in innovative outcomes.[22] Andrew Hargadon, professor at University of California, Davis, advocates a type of cross-pollination he calls "technology brokering."[23] This involves assembling people from different social structures and cultures into new combinations. Research conducted for his book *How Breakthroughs Happen* found that there is more to creating insights and innovating than "designing the innovative organization, picking creative people, and keeping them happy."[24] He argues that innovation is a social process of reassembling people, ideas, and objects in new combinations.

Substitute *life brokering* for *technology brokering,* and it is clear that innovation applies as much to solving life challenges as it does to addressing work challenges. Insights emerge from creating new recipes from existing ingredients combined in new ways, and it requires strategic curiosity to put those insights to work to create and inspire beneficial change.

Insights that come from cross-pollinating precede innovation. Whether to focus on the quantity or quality of insights and innovation takes curious exploration. Both quantity and quality are important, but perhaps for different goals. This has to do with a difference between breakthrough insights and innovations versus smaller, incremental ones. So does cross-pollinating to generate large quantities of ideas necessarily translate into the highest quality? Although the financial returns of innovations are not always a measure of the value they have for your life, it is an interesting way to look more closely at the benefit of cross-pollination.

Lee Fleming's research on more than seventeen thousand patents suggests that the financial value of innovations resulting from cross-pollination is actually lower, on average, than the financial value of innovations coming from more homogenous groups.[25] He suggests that the wider the distance between the backgrounds and disciplines of team members, the lower the financial return of the average innovation. What? Does this mean that cross-pollinating provides less value than sticking with our own kind? The short answer is: no.

Fleming's findings shed light on a particularly interesting benefit of cross-pollination that dumps us right back into being remarkable and busting through stagnation to do good stuff. He found that cross-pollinating, multidisciplinary work does result in far more breakthrough insights and innovations...and far more blunders. It's a difference between average results (from homogenous interactions) and outcomes that bust out of average (from cross-pollination). In the world of finance, this relates to the difference between high alpha (growth) and high beta (volatility)—referring to the trade-off between risk and reward.

Similar → Predictable
Different → Remarkable

If you're only looking for moderate and ordinary innovation, cross-pollination may not be your best bet. Pairing yourself with less-aligned people and ideas is risky because assumptions are so different. Busting assumptions, however, is central to the Living Curiously Method, so going for bigger ideas and innovations is your best chance to be remarkable. The payoff makes adventuring in the blunder-prone world of cross-pollination worthwhile. Also, as you'll later see, blundering has tremendous value.

Enhancing Your Adventures with Insights
When you live curiously, adventure can happen anywhere—the strip mall during back-to-school sales, the dive bar on a rainy day, the ancient bazaar during civil unrest, or the bat-filled island cave during typhoon season. Adventure can happen with anyone—the server who shares stories of mysterious sake festivals in Japan, the Thai professor you meet at a Bangkok food stand who shows you hidden sites, the woman you meet in line at the airport who invites you to dinner at her crowded home in Lima, or the vendor at the farmers' market who moonlights as a dominatrix. This I know.

Cross-pollinating is great training for being able to have rational conversations with people you disagree with. With applied curiosity, it will also reduce the number of people you don't understand (yet). You may be as astonished as I have been when you see how adventures appear before you as you surprise people by being genuinely curious when they expect to shock you—it's like an invitation to adventure.

Cross-pollinating fueled by curiosity uncovers insights that often remain hidden. You are the only person in the world who can experience the combination of any adventure and *you*. When you strategically collide with fear-inducing and intrigue-inducing people and places with the purpose of exploring, your life will never be without insight-infused adventure.

The cross-pollination that the Living Curiously Method advocates might become second nature to you, like it has to me. It creates a type of purposefully curious lifestyle where the treasure chest of adventure lies around every corner and insights are there for the taking...all you have to do is be intrigued and brave enough to open the chest.

" *The big question is whether you are going to be able to say a hearty yes to your adventure.* —JOSEPH CAMPBELL

Getting Smarter

Although we love to romanticize our history and business super-heroes (while secretly dreaming of becoming one), Hargadon argues that breakthrough innovation cannot be attributed to "lone geniuses." This is a powerful case for judging compassionately and for understanding that cross-pollination is valuable with all kinds of people, not just noted geniuses and highly accomplished folk. Good ideas don't care who they happen to, but they seem to happen to a collective *us*. Perhaps cross-pollination is how we become geniuses together.

When we reach out to create opportunities for direct interactions with a variety of people (making an effort to collide), we move beyond being stuck primarily with information extracted from abstracts, made up by bloggers, or misreported by less-than-thorough journalists. Sticking to information that comes from similar sources keeps us stuck comfortably finding information that we want to believe in the first place—it's another pesky cognitive bias (this one's called confirmation bias, to be exact). How often do our "trusted sources" feed us information that we have already deemed tasty enough to consume? If that information is wrong, we're less likely to see it as such because we want to believe what our sources say. When you curiously explore how chunks of knowledge from one industry, field, or culture enhance or contradict a chunk of knowledge from another, though, the world opens up—you get smarter. Cross-pollination provides knowledge beyond our comfort zone, helping us to understand more by exposing that we may know less.

So often it's the fear of looking dumb that prevents us from getting smarter. The crazy thing is that it's only when we finally realize how little we know that we actually become smarter.

" *The cross pollination of disciplines is fundamental to truly revolutionary advances in our culture.*
—Neil deGrasse Tyson

How do you use cross-pollination to produce life-changing insights and breakthrough innovations to help you do good stuff in the world? Leave your comfort zone and cross-pollinate. After eleven years in an orphanage, that's exactly what Dan Ross did. Here is his story.

Can Breaking Rules Save a Ruler?

Dan's comfort zone was the five-block radius around the orphanage in Brooklyn where he lived for the first eleven years of his life. He still vividly remembers the mysterious nurses, the stories he read when he snuck and borrowed copies of their *True Confessions* magazine, and his constant state of curiosity about the world outside his tiny universe. The *True Confessions* stories Dan secretly snatched were where he first learned the concept of a kiss. The idea that touching lips with someone was something secret and could cause one to "feel good" was a complete mystery to him. He continued to feed his unusually intense curiosity with books and magazines. These secondhand sources were his windows to the world.

By the time Dan was eleven years old, the Great Depression had contributed to a dire financial situation at the orphanage. It was determined that every orphan with any living family member, however remotely related, would be dropped off with that relative. Dan was taken by subway to the Bronx, where he was unceremoniously deposited at the tenement apartment of the man who was his father.

Many would describe this life event as traumatic. More than eighty years later, Dan described that first subway ride as the beginning of finding a more satisfying way to address his intense curiosity — of finally seeing how the private world of life between the pages of books and magazines could become a world of real possibilities for him. He began to dream.

"I found my big life change to be fascinating," Dan told me. "It made me more curious than anything else. In my old world, the orphanage was completely regimented and authoritative. We were told when to eat, when to sleep...when to do everything, and suddenly that was replaced with different people, with no rules and no discipline. I could meet anyone and go wherever I wanted. And I wanted. And I went."

After a lifetime of confinement, Dan set out to supplement his appetite for reading with the firsthand experience of meeting as many people and exposing himself to as many intriguing opportunities as possible. His constant exploring landed him in the Bethlehem Steel shipyards, where he used his curiosity, natural mechanical proclivity, and Dale Carnegie's *How to Win Friends and Influence People* (his "bible") to become the youngest person to achieve the highest-level electrician status in the yard.

"I was always curious. Always," Dan explained.

Soon Dan had fallen in love, married Marion, and had a baby. The American Dream seemed within his grasp. "With a pregnant wife and a toddler, I was doing the responsible thing and working in trucking. It brought me financial stability, but I hated trucking. You know that kind of curiosity where you feel there's something more just beyond your grasp? Well, you know those ads they have on the subway? On my way home from work, I looked up, and one of the ads was speaking to me. It said, 'Television Needs You.' Television was just getting started, and I had this intriguing feeling, so I signed up before even looking into whether there would be a job for me when I finished the [training] course."

Dan completed the television course only to find out that in New York there were no jobs in television for anyone without special connections. He had none. With his eight-month-pregnant wife's blessing and the last of their money, Dan leaned into his considerable fear and set out for Hollywood. His intention was to give himself four days to get a job in television. He had no backup plan.

Of the three major television networks, only NBC had no union contract, so Dan started there. Although he didn't know it at the time, Dan had landed in Hollywood at the dawn of television. In the transition from radio to live television broadcasting, the head of NBC television had just received orders to hire trained electricians to rig the old radio studio into a television studio. Dan, strategically ignoring directions to mail in his application, had coincidentally flown across the country and walked straight into NBC headquarters on that very same day.

With a few dollars left to his name, Dan called Marion and told her that the family would soon be moving to Los Angeles because he was heading over to Sunset and Vine to Radio City West, where he would begin to make a life by creating television.

"I met and worked with all the greats: Bing Crosby, Groucho Marx, Jack Paar, Dinah Shore, Milton Berle, Dean Martin, Steve Allen, Bob Hope, Ronnie Reagan; Nancy Reagan even made me a sandwich once."

After several years working in television, Dan got his biggest break when he was called away from the set of *Days of Our Lives* to help with an emergency on the set of Johnny Carson's show. Dan had a solid gig, but the opportunity to meet new people and work on new sets intrigued him enough to risk his stable job.

Johnny had reluctantly agreed to move from the New York studio to Los Angeles so it would be easier to book LA-based guest stars. But it wasn't working. There were lighting problems in the LA studio, and no matter how many lighting electricians they cycled through, none were getting it right. Johnny was increasingly frustrated, and there were huge financial implications too. RCA owned NBC, and as NBC's biggest property, Johnny Carson was the ruler of the network. If the LA move didn't pay off, well, Johnny Carson's show — and the network's West Coast venture — could have been ruined.

"The first day I was on the set, I saw that the lighting guys were doing everything by the book. I also saw that it wasn't working. The lighting delays were interrupting Johnny's flow. I was a proud union guy, but I learned from the orphanage and the shipyards that you gotta apply curiosity to know when to follow the rules and when to break them." And that's what Dan did. "I would never work for free, but I had to come in early and off the clock to do what had to be done. The lighting was all set up according to the electrician union's manual, but it wasn't going to work for Johnny. I unhooked everything and rerigged the entire system. Sure, I was afraid, because if it didn't work, I knew that not only would I be fired, I would probably never work in television again. What I didn't know at the time was that if it didn't work, we would have also lost Johnny's show, and the whole future of the studio would have been in jeopardy."

Dan had learned to question his own strongly held assumption that the union was always right. In doing so, he was able to change a system that hadn't allowed Johnny Carson to maintain his comedic flow without stopping and starting to adjust the lights. It worked. Dan's seemingly small way of doing good stuff saved *The Johnny Carson Show*. Perhaps even more importantly, the right lighting allowed Johnny to maintain his signature humor style and to spontaneously call successful stand-up comics to the famed couch.

It has been said that one of the biggest influences on whether a stand-up comedian's career took off was being on Johnny Carson's *Tonight Show* and being called to the couch. This honor changed the trajectory of many stand-up comics' careers, including Eddie Murphy, Jerry Seinfeld, Ellen DeGeneres, and Drew Carey.

Dan's curiosity and willingness to cross-pollinate by leaning into situations that induced fear and intrigue taught him what was necessary to overcome stagnation in the television industry. Dan's contribution might have seemed like a small act of good, but the ripple effect averted cancelation of a wildly successful show and paved the road for amazing things for the television industry—all out of the remarkably adventurous life of an orphan from Brooklyn. Dan spent the rest of his career as Johnny Carson's chief electrician and was ultimately honored by the Television Academy.

Lubrication

Exercise 3.1: Shake Up Your Thoughts

This exercise will shake up your thoughts so you can get the most from cross-pollinating opportunities.

1. Elevate curiosity.
2. Schedule 5 minutes of iconoclastic[26] thought each day. This requires you to challenge your cherished beliefs (spiritual, political, or other) and the key institutions you respect—but only for 5 minutes and only in your own mind. If this makes you feel guilty for questioning what you've been trained to accept, try to replace guilt with curiosity. Give yourself another bonus point because this is hard.
3. Map out formal and informal collaboration opportunities. Write down ideas for formal and chance meetings, parties, volunteer projects, meet ups, and active social media groups.

4. Commit to a way to document your random ideas and practices. For example, plan a specific way and place to document what you learn as you delve into interesting books, new science, different political ideas, ancient philosophies, future technologies, unusual cultures, newly revealed historical events, and different things to think about. I like the old-timey shoebox-with-note-cards method.

5. Prime yourself to go wild by creating associations while cross-pollinating. For example:

   cause and effect (itch → scratch)
   resemblance (banana → yellow)
   categories (technology →software)[27]

   These associations will help you recognize insights that others may miss.

6. Get comfortable with rejection—it will not kill you. Practice rejection by asking for a discount the next time you buy a cocktail, coffee, or tea; by asking to get a free upgrade the next time you fly; or by asking the manager of a big-box store if you can make an announcement over the loudspeaker. Some rejection and blundering will happen in the Method, but these will give you rejection calluses…and more opportunities to be curious.

There are three general blockages that prevent cross-pollinating:

- Not knowing what people and experiences to seek out
- Not knowing when cross-pollinating opportunities are right in front of you
- Not understanding how to be brave enough to replace intimidation with thrill

The next exercises will help you address all three of these blockages. But first, it's important to know the difference between fear and phobia.

❝ *Everything that irritates us about others can lead us to an understanding of ourselves.* —C. G. Jung

The Difference between Fear and Phobia

The Living Curiously Method makes a very clear distinction between fear-inducing and phobia-inducing scenarios. The fear you feel by meeting with and exposing yourself to people and experiences you're afraid of should never be so hard-core as to induce a phobia. Think about this being fun and enriching, and inducing no more than an eyebrow-plucking level of discomfort. For example, if your fear of cross-pollinating with a noted artist or a high-level politician is caused by intimidation, this is an acceptable level of fear to challenge. If your fear arises because someone or something could cause psychological or bodily harm, this is not an acceptable level of fear to experience in order to cross-pollinate.

According to Dr. R. Reid Wilson, spokesman for the American Psychological Association and author of the book *Don't Panic*, fear and phobia are different but related.[28] A phobia is an intense fear that causes physical and/or psychological impairment. Phobia could be considered fear's more persistent and impactful cousin.

Reflection

Exercise 3.2: Collide with Fear-Inducing People and Places
Complete the following statements for yourself, and as you do so, be curious about where your fear comes from. It can be helpful to know that the kind of fear that often blocks us from meeting people is actually only intimidation. Screw that. What's the worst that can happen?

Commit to inducing a level of fear that is reasonable for you. This isn't a psychological experiment, and it should not be torturous. It's a way to curiously identify untapped opportunities for cross-pollination. If you are part of a team or mastermind group, once you have completed these statements for yourself, feel free to share…or you can keep them private.

1. People who are into _____ scare me.
2. I would never want to visit _____ because I am afraid I would _____.
3. I'm not the kind of person who would fit in _____.
4. The _____ that believe _____ make me uncomfortable.
5. People who say stupid things like _____ make me _____.
6. If I hang around _____, I'm afraid that I'll start to _____.
7. I would love to have _____ adventure, but _____.
8. I'm not _____ enough to ask the right questions of or interact with _____.
9. People who have achieved _____ would never relate to me because I'm _____.
10. People who have never achieved _____ would never relate to me because I'm _____.
11. I don't know much about _____, but I have no reason to subject myself to ideas about _____.
12. I'm afraid that _____ people will just try to exploit me for my _____.
13. I would love to meet and interview people who have achieved _____, but I don't know what I'd ask or offer.

The fear of the number thirteen is called triskaidekaphobia, so if you have that fear, answer all thirteen questions. If you have that phobia, skip one.

Exercise 3.3: And Now...Make Some Lists

Now that you've identified your fears and perhaps even where some of them come from, it's time to push your boundaries a bit to cross-pollinate.

1. Inspired by your statements about fear-inducing people and places, create a list of at least 5 specific people whom you're curious to meet. In addition to the general titles, this list should include specific names. Look around your everyday life to write this list. You can also conduct research to come up with specific names. Elevating curiosity will help you write down the best names for productive cross-pollinating.

   Be sure not to dismiss people you encounter in your daily life. Perceived power is not a measure of the value that cross-pollinating provides. However, do not let fear stop you from attempting to meet high-powered or famous people if that's the type of cross-pollination that will help you. The barriers to meeting people are virtually nonexistent if you're brave or persistent enough. There are very few limits to your ability to attempt to connect. The secret is that even when you're unsuccessful in your attempts to collide with certain people, the collisions you experience in the attempt often provide the cross-pollination you really need. Accidental collisions are valuable too.

2. Now make a list of 5 places that you're curious to visit. Think locally, globally, and even virtually.

   You don't have to be wealthy to have adventure. Adventures that inspire can be discovered in familiar as well as distant places. Finding and experiencing the mystique in the mundane has no price tag. This is the exact skill that will help you find inspiration in your own neighborhood as well as on world travels, both real and virtual.

These exercises are meant to help you start generating your lists of people and places for cross-pollinating. They will also prepare you to maximize the benefits of cross-pollinating. As you do this, it's fine to have the goal to simply learn as much as you can about as much as you can. That's actually one of my favorite goals. It's also great to apply these exercises toward your specific world-benefitting goal.

Here's an example of how parts of Exercises 3.2 and 3.3 might look when completed with a specific goal in mind. Let's say your goal is to make the schools in your district safer.

- People who <u>are into guns and the National Rifle Association</u> scare me (statement 1).
- People who have never achieved <u>consensus with diverse</u> groups could never relate to me because I'm <u>staunchly pro–gun control and I need to work with anti–gun control proponents</u> (statement 10).
- I don't know much about <u>gun technology,</u> but I have no reason to subject myself to ideas about <u>the tactics of bounty hunters</u> (statement 11).
- I would love to meet and interview people who have achieved <u>successfully opening schools in challenging places like Afghanistan,</u> but I don't know what I'd ask or offer (statement 13).

This can seem a bit random or clunky, but it will stimulate ideas of people to meet. In this example, your statements might inspire you to write down the names of the people associated with these titles:

- The local head of the NRA
- A gun shop owner who is pro–gun control
- An international authority on education
- A gun lobbyist
- A weapons specialist

- A school principal who supports having concealed weapons on school grounds—and one who is vehemently opposed
- A head of a foundation for a school for girls in Afghanistan
- A best-selling author who writes psychological novels
- A noted architect who specializes in museum security
- Someone starting a school in a war zone
- Your grocery clerk from Pakistan

Who else can you think of?

Now that you've taken the first steps to prepare to collide with fear-inducing people and places, it will be easier to stop fear from getting in the way of colliding with *intrigue*-inducing people and places. Give yourself two to five bonus points if you find overlap between what induces fear and what induces intrigue.

I know there are a lot of exercises in this cross-pollinating step of the Method. Don't give up. Sure, tackling them all in order will give you the most comprehensive cross-pollinating experiences (and you can sneak yourself a few extra bonus points). But you still get to give yourself a good grade even if you don't try them all in the first pass, because you'll be a better cross-pollinator after completing just some of the exercises. Once you get the hang of it with the first few exercises, cross-pollinating will start to become natural. It will also be its own adventure.

Exercise 3.4: Collide with Intrigue-Inducing People and Places

Reflection

What effortlessly arouses your curiosity? Intrigue is mysterious and personal. Intrigue, like arousal, is one of the most powerful persuasive emotions. It is different from, but not uncommonly related to, fear.

Tap your curiosity and then complete these statements for yourself. If and when applicable, this is also a fun exercise to complete with your coworkers, friends, or mastermind group if you have one.

1. I have always wondered about the subject of _____, but I haven't explored it as much as I would like because of _____.
2. I cannot understand why so many people find _____ interesting when I would rather spend time with _____.
3. I'm really interested in _____, but I'm not _____ enough to have pursued this interest in the past.
4. I should really spend more time exposing myself to the field of _____, but I _____.
5. My interest in _____ embarrasses me.
6. I wouldn't want _____ to know that I am interested in _____.
7. If I had to learn _____ to do what I really feel I'm meant to do, I think _____.
8. Privately, I'm interested in _____; publicly, I'm interested in _____.
9. Although I wouldn't want my friends or coworkers to know, the one area that I should know more about in order to really excel is _____.
10. I'm curious about people who _____, and I wonder how they _____.
11. If I could have any adventure, it would be to explore the _____ culture.
12. I don't really ever interact with people in the circus because they don't seem to have anything in common with us, but I suppose we have more in common with them than we do with people in _____.
13. Why do _____ believe _____?

You can complete these statements randomly and they will still work, but here's an example of how you might complete the statements if you are specifically relating this exercise to what you're doing to benefit the world. You might be surprised.

Let's say Arjun is working on water purification innovation. He has developed a very portable water purification system. He thinks it could have a huge impact because it eliminates toxins from stagnant water in a totally new and relatively inexpensive way. He doesn't know the politics of local or global purification efforts, nor does he know what would be the best initial market for the product. He grew up in India in a village where clean water was a luxury for many, and he remembers his neighbors trudging miles for access to clean water. (Did you see Steps 1 and 2 of the Method there? Good, you're catching on!) Here's what some of his statements might look like.

- I'm really interested in <u>meteorology</u>, but I'm not <u>connected</u> enough to have pursued this interest in the past (statement 3).
- My interest in <u>sewage</u> embarrasses me (statement 5).
- If I had to learn <u>how to start a nonprofit organization or B Corp</u> to do what I really feel I'm meant to do, <u>I think I would first have to get a position on a nonprofit board</u> (statement 7).
- I'm curious about people who are <u>involved in politics</u>, and I wonder how they <u>maintain their ethics and values</u> (statement 10).

Random, huh? Can you see a way to relate Arjun's statements to his goal? There is no one right answer. It's challenging and requires curiosity. That's the point of cross-pollination—it can seem random and fuzzy, until the insights that are revealed and the ideas that are generated come into focus. They will.

" *If you don't know where you are going, you might wind up someplace else.* —YOGI BERRA

Propulsion

Exercise 3.5: And Now...Add to Your Lists
You kept those lists from Exercise 3.3 in a safe place, right?
Now go back and add to them.

1. Based on your answers in Exercise 3.4, add 5 intrigue-inducing people to your previous list of 5 fear-inducing people.
2. Add 5 new intrigue-inducing places to your previous list of 5 places.
3. Once you have lists of 10 people and 10 places, make a list of 5 topics you would like to learn more about or 5 skills you'd like to acquire. Feel free to use some of the knowledge gaps you identified in Step 1 of the Method, or you can use new ideas generated from these exercises. There are endless trails for curiosity.
4. Set the three lists aside.

You may be tempted now to set the Method aside and think about things that are easier to think about. That's cool, but wait! Before you do, commit to the exact time and date you'll come back to jumping into the next exercises. The world needs your remarkability and the good stuff you'll do.

The next exercises will show you how to connect seemingly random people, places, and topics to create curious questions that will turn your cross-pollinating into adventure and insights.

> " *Do stuff. Be clenched, curious. Not waiting for inspiration's shove or society's kiss on your forehead. Pay attention. It's all about paying attention. Attention is vitality. It connects you with others. It makes you eager. Stay eager.*
> —SUSAN SONTAG

Exercise 3.6: Play Dress-Up for Your Mind

1. Every day for a week, choose a different perspective to embody for at least 15 minutes. Here is a list to help you consider different perspectives:
    - astronaut
    - professional athlete
    - street artist
    - seven-year-old
    - musician
    - real estate developer
    - architect
    - drag queen
    - refugee
    - aid worker
    - fashion designer
    - chemist
    - reality show personality
    - venture capitalist
    - cancer researcher
    - motivational speaker
    - exonerated convict
    - florist
    - migrant farmer
    - stand-up comedian

    Hint: By elevating curiosity, you can mentally move away from how *you* think your temporary perspective would see the world and toward how *they* might actually see the world. More insights will flow into your life.

2. During your perspective-taking week, for at least 15 minutes each day, go exploring from your temporarily adopted perspective. If you're able to get outside and walk, do that. Pay attention and stay eager. Actively find things to interest you from your new perspective. Try to keep your mind away from

things you normally think about. You'll be getting perspicacious while you perspire.

Hint: Perspective taking and empathy are different. Perspective taking is mentally seeing the world from a different viewpoint, whereas empathy is the ability to connect with others emotionally. Perspective taking results in greater insights. Research conducted by Adam Galinsky et al. at Northwestern's Kellogg School of Management showed that perspective taking increases the ability to discover hidden agreements in order to achieve successful negotiations,[29] while empathy did not aid with this ability and is, at times, detrimental to achieving successful negotiations.

3. Look over your lists of people, places, and topics and create a list of related, curious questions that come to mind during your week of walkabouts.

Playing dress-up for your mind is something you can do from anywhere. It's being purposeful about creating inspiring adventures.

> **"** *Adventure is worthwhile in itself.* —AMELIA EARHART

Now you have your four lists:

1. Fear-inducing and intrigue-inducing people
2. Fear-inducing and intrigue-inducing places
3. New topics, subjects, or skills to pursue
4. Curious questions

Exercise 3.6 Adjunct: Goals

As an adjunct to exercise 3.6, here are three goals:

1. Contact all the people from List 1 and meet the majority of them (in person or virtually) within the next 12 months. Meeting these people virtually could probably be accomplished in less than 12 hours, so...

2. Plan to visit (physically or virtually) all of the places from List 2 (include actual dates in your plans) and visit at least half of the places within the next 12 months. If you're worried that this requires resources you don't have, I promise that living curiously has no financial requirements. If you can only visit by researching in a book or visiting virtually, that will work.

3. Make cross-pollinating a lifelong adventure.

Dear and Pleasant Strangers

In addition to your collision goals for the next year, there will be ample opportunities to cross-pollinate in your everyday life. Talk to strangers. When you aim to collide with famous or powerful people, sometimes you'll be rejected, but if you're ready for unintended cross-pollinating collisions with other people along the way, you'll be amazed at what you learn. Talking to strangers prepares you for this.

If you're like most people—still figuring out the specifics of how you'll make and inspire beneficial change—you can use the topics, subjects, or skills that you identified on List 3 as explanation for contacting the people and visiting the places on your lists. It's too bad that as adults, we can't contact people and places by simply explaining that we're working on a school project...or can we? Again, when I've explained that I'm working on living curiously and have some curious questions that they are uniquely qualified to answer, people rarely say no. Ask like that, or say you're asking out of curiosity.

Your list of curious questions will turn places to visit into things to do, but before you jump into that, make your first to-do answering your curious questions. Your curious questions from List 4 will help guide your conversations and experiences. The good news is that creating curious questions is like working out at the gym—you'll grow your curiosity "muscle" so that you'll find it easier and easier to keep adding to that list of curious questions. Easily generating curious questions is one of the many benefits of living curiously.

While asking curious questions generates more curious questions, cross-pollinating builds your networks to create more cross-pollinating opportunities. Let's face it, when you're interested in other people, you will be more interesting. Don't believe it? Try hanging out with someone who has zero interest in you. On the flip side, try enjoying a party where your singular focus is to follow your curiosity about people, and watch your networks expand organically and genuinely.

Expanding your social circles with greater diversity is a good thing, because the wider the diversity in your social circle, the more you're going to hear and learn about stuff. There is a lot of science behind this, but it's pretty obvious even without the vast research that proves it. Fascinating studies show that social circles affect our weight, smoking behavior, and happiness on a personal level, and even our ability to detect contagious outbreaks on a societal level.[30] Cross-pollinating expands our social circles, which in turn, provides greater opportunities for cross-pollinating.

As you continue to learn a lot about a lot, you'll generate even more insights when you mix, match, and put pieces of that knowledge together. Zigzagging is one way to do that.

> ### Exercise 3.7: Practice Zigzagging
> Zigzagging is connecting seemingly unconnected people, places, lessons, experiences, facts, and challenges to uncover the innovations, insights, and inspiring adventure that most people miss. Zigzagging is a skill that takes practice. It allows you to take what you learn from cross-pollinating and use it to create connections that increase your body of knowledge. See? It will actually make you smarter. I often zigzag in my mind. Sometimes I involve other people.

Lubrication

❝ *In order for us to truly create and contribute to the world, we have to be able to connect countless dots, to cross-pollinate ideas from a wealth of disciplines, to combine and recombine these pieces and build new castles.* —Maria Popova

1. Pick a random person, a random place, and a random topic, or have someone pick these for you. For example, the last time I asked my son to pick these for me, this is what I got: Betty, the nail salon lady who remembers everyone's name; Central Park; and food trucks.
2. Think creatively or actually research the person, place, and topic. Take notes, think in metaphors, concentrate on small and large details, and remove mental constraints by thinking preposterously.
3. Take what you learned and zigzag connections between the seemingly unrelated person, place, and topic. The connections will often only occur in the tiniest of details, but they are always there if you look for them.

Using the example provided by my son, I asked famed publicist Joanne McCall[31] to have a go at zigzagging without the benefit of time, research, or even much thought. She is brilliant at connecting current events and stuff the media is interested in to her clients' content. It took her about forty-seven seconds, and here is what she came up with:

Central Park reminds me of the time I hooked my TRX straps to a fence in the park to exercise. TRX is a form of exercise invented by a Navy SEAL, and the Central Park adventure was part of my boot camp group challenge to exercise in crazy places. It was hilarious and so much fun.

This made me think of seeing the food cart in the park and of hearing all the different sounds from the tourists and their different languages. This made me think of the colorful sights and sounds of the nail salon. Exercise trends, food trends, nail trends...this makes me curious about how they all relate.

See? Zigzagging is a great private mental exercise or a fun one to do with others. You can even take two unrelated topics and try zigzagging like this.

What Do Punk Rock and Circuit Boards Have in Common?

Zigzagging requires strategically applying curiosity to find tiny similarities in seemingly random things...like punk rock and circuit boards, for example. Musically, most punk rock strives to simplify and strip the music down to just the essential elements to communicate its messages with no distracting flourishes like random flute solos. Similarly, in circuit board design, the goal is to simplify and strip down the elements so only the most critical remain and there is no extraneous cost or distortion to the circuit signal.

> **"** *When scientists are asked what they are working on, their response is seldom 'Finding the origin of the universe' or 'Seeking to cure cancer.' Usually, they will claim to be tackling a very specific problem—a small piece of the jigsaw that builds up the big picture.... No scientist makes a unique contribution.*
> —MARTIN REES, PRESIDENT OF THE ROYAL SOCIETY

Cross-pollinating is a vital part of living curiously, and zigzagging is how you'll maximize the curious questions and insights so they build exponentially. These insights fuel innovation, enhance adventure, make you smarter, and help you figure out cool things to do with your life. Once you're comfortable and gaining the incredible benefits of cross-pollinating, you might be curious how best to connect with your collisions. Start by asking yourself this question: Can one be interesting without being interested? Give yourself another bonus point for your answer, and three more for being ready to take the next step.

Step 4: Find Uncommon Commonalities

" *The one thing that unites all human beings, regardless of age, gender, religion, economic status, or ethnic background, is that, deep down inside, we all believe that we are above-average drivers.* —DAVE BARRY

It's time to dip our toes into sexy mind science. This step is a connection and influence tool deeply rooted in the science of persuasion, influence, and sales. It is a vital step in the Living Curiously Method, and it will become clear that it is also power-ful in many aspects of your life. I love this step because it's like a treasure hunt. I hope you enjoy it too.

There are two stages in Step 4, and they both involve inter-acting with humans. Feel free to grab your lists from Step 3 or pick new humans.

1. Connect with unusual things loved in common
2. Connect with unusual things hated in common

Together, I call them finding uncommon commonalities.

Key Benefits

There are three key benefits to finding uncommon commonalities:

- Persuading ethically and having more influence
- Being more helpful
- Navigating the connection economy

Persuading Ethically and Having More Influence

It's okay if you're thinking, *I don't sell. I don't need to persuade or influence. It's not my job, and it's not what I like to do.* You may even think that persuasion and selling sound manipulative. When they're done wrong, you're absolutely right. Sales can be manipulative. So if you're a liar, stop here and do good by gifting this book to someone honest and with good intentions.

Sales done right, however, results in the exchange of resources that leaves both you and your buyer better off in the end. That is not slimy—it is nothing short of noble. I call this way of noble selling "arousing the buy curious."

Arousing the buy curious uses the sexy mind science of ethical persuasion and the power of curiosity. The vast majority of what we say and do involves some attempt to entice, convince, arouse, cajole, persuade, influence, or sell. Sometimes it's subtle and part of the texture of a conversation or action. Sometimes it's the blatant reason for the conversation or action. Either way, the ability to do this is as critical to our happiness as it is to our survival. If your service, product, or mission is important and beneficial, you owe it to yourself and to your beneficiaries to be convincing. Doing good stuff may start with you alone, but it rarely ends with you alone.

Bonus benefit: Understanding how to arouse the buy curious in this noble way also allows you to spot and avoid when you're being sold in a manipulative way.

Being More Helpful

First, you will get curious *about* others. You'll investigate: what do we have in common? Next, you will arouse curiosity *in* others. When you arouse curiosity in others, the key questions they should be asking are: What does this mean? What does this mean for me? You don't have to answer this for them. If you can facilitate their own discovery of answers to these questions, you can stand by as the beneficent benefactor. That's kind of superheroish—it's certainly remarkable—and very helpful of you. When their answers are aligned with your goals for doing good stuff, you have a powerful ally.

Navigating the Connection Economy

> **❝** *Each and every person has an unlimited ability to achieve anything he or she wants through the power of connection.*
> —SETH GODIN

It may be obvious, but there is also vast scientific evidence that indicates that we feel most connected to people who are similar to us. Studies even suggest that we're more likely to help others who share our same values, age, sex, birthday, and name.[32] If your last name is Ginsberg or Saltzman, I won't be able to resist helping you with your remarkable project. Try me. It is easier to connect with people that are obviously like us, and that's okay. However, this comfort of connection is why active cross-pollinating with people not so obviously like us is vital if we want to also gain the insights and adventure that hide outside our comfort zone.

Powerful connections come from finding uncommon commonalities, and the more connected we are, the more likely we are to persuade and be persuaded to do good stuff. The more this hunt for uncommon commonalities becomes part of your everyday interactions, the wider your connection network will become, and the more allies you'll have.

Commonalities versus Uncommon Commonalities
Why is it more powerful when the things we share in common are uncommon? Think about seeing an acquaintance on the street in Dallas, Texas, just north of your hometown of Austin. Both of you are wearing the identical T-shirt with University of Texas's Hook 'em Horns on the front. Maybe you nod and smile at one another. Maybe not. The commonality of being a supporter of the

same college is a point of connection, but it's not that uncommon near the college. Now think about bumping into that same acquaintance wearing that same T-shirt on the street in Amsterdam. You're probably far more likely to meet for a beer or at a coffee shop in Amsterdam. Your connection will be stronger.

All commonalities provide connections. When our connections and bonds are stronger, our power of influence and persuasion is greater. Finding *uncommon* commonalities isn't always easy, but when you make an effort to investigate, you can always find them. Start with this goal. Guillaume Schaer has made it his goal to find commonalities among the widest range of people from around the world. Here is his story.

Can Teddy Bears Fund Adventures?

When Guillaume was seven years old, he ceremoniously announced to his family that his plan was to travel the world — and fly planes. Before he was old enough to drive a car, Guillaume was flying himself around the country.

He was passionately curious about how different people in different cultures adapt to different environments in similar ways. He was interested in finding uncommon commonalities. This curiosity, combined with his interest in how computers aid that adaptation, directed Guillaume into a career at the intersection of engineering and travel. He became a security expert who was flown around the world to work on secretive projects with exotic code names.

I wasn't the only one whose curiosity was piqued by the secrecy of his work. He told me, "No matter how many tricky situations you encounter traveling around the world, when you get pulled aside after your passport mysteriously beeps as it's being scanned by the US Customs officer, your mind starts racing; a bit of panic creeps in. I knew that I couldn't explain the reason for the Russian stamp on my passport from the prior month any more than I could explain why I was in the US headed to Oak Ridge, Tennessee. I had to find different ways to navigate these tricky situations."

No matter how many cocktails I ordered, I couldn't tempt Guillaume to share the details of the security projects he has worked on, but he did explain that getting out of tricky situations usually involved finding something in common with very different, and often suspicion-filled, people. He also let slip that the Oak Ridge, Tennessee, project was at the Y-12 National Security Complex, which was built as part of the Manhattan Project for enriching uranium for the first atomic bombs. It is now operated as a production and maintenance facility for uranium parts for nuclear weapons. You can imagine that it's a pretty suspicion-filled place.

When he wasn't traveling for work, Guillaume looked for ways to combine his interest in technology, travel, and doing good stuff in the world. As an expert travel hacker, he combined all three of these interests as often as he could—like the time he shipped teddy bears to children's hospitals throughout the United States as part of a travel hacking plan for an amazing trip to Brazil.

"I was used to finding things that people had in common. This time I wanted to find a common thread that connected two different goals—to do good and to have an adventure," he told me. By shipping teddy bears around the United States, he not only brought joy to children in hospitals but also racked up airline miles for a flight to Brazil. Talk about a connection economy!

After years of security work in the bowels of remote buildings, he decided to stay closer to his wonderful wife and darling daughter and to use his experience to help people with their online businesses and travel adventures. Guillaume learned that finding commonalities was just as much a part of how he could understand people for security work as it was for helping his customers connect with their customers.

"Wherever you go, you see that people are seeking to figure out the same things: how to learn, how to love, and how to leave a trace of having ever existed," Guillaume explained. "When you work in an industry that is full of suspicion and distrust, it's important to check yourself so you can be curious before you judge. As humans we have so much in common, but sometimes we have to actively look for it in order to connect. The most powerful commonalities are often uncommon; there are always ways to connect if you really look. I love helping people create these connections online and through experiencing the world."

Guillaume's life and adventures have helped him learn from

the similarities in the rainforests of Brazil and the desert of Algeria, in the fjords of Greenland and the beaches of Goa, and in the plains of the Serengeti and the mountains of China. His travels have expanded his search for cultural commonalities in the sound of tango in Buenos Aires and fado music in Lisbon, and in the smell of tulips in the Netherlands and spices in Zanzibar. No matter how disparate the locations and exotic the experiences, the process of actively seeking uncommon commonalities has provided Guillaume the most amazing opportunities to connect with the most diverse people.

Through his company, IdeaLiftOff,[33] he helps people and companies get ideas off the ground. He continues to work on incorporating technology to help others create and experience inspiring, curiosity-driven adventures to connect people from around the world. He also teaches others how they can do good stuff while living adventurous lives.

Are You Ready for This?

Yeah, you are. The first three steps of the Living Curiously Method have prepared you for finding uncommon commonalities in very specific ways.

1. Starting with what you're not highlighted areas to explore commonalities that are often less obvious and, therefore, potentially less common. For example, let's say you and the person with whom you want to connect both do development work abroad but not work that supports, promotes, or is affiliated with any religion. Your message is not for religious missionaries, even though most of the other development organizations in the area are religiously affiliated. That provides an uncommon commonality.

2. Dumpster-diving your life identified conversations and experiences that, although unique to you, have interesting commonalities to dig out. For example, maybe you and the person with whom you want to connect both had professional athlete parents who dragged you to baseball games…and you both dislike baseball. That's an uncommon commonality.

3. Cross-pollinating identified people with whom you want to connect. For example, you were fearful (and maybe even intrigued) to meet a very successful speaker who is an ex–drug dealer. You want to convince her to contribute to your training program on unusual forms of entrepreneurship. Interest in unusual forms of entrepreneurship is an uncommon commonality.

Lubrication

Exercise 4.1: Prepare to Persuade
Before you dive into the pool with everyone you're curious about, do a little preparation for your connecting desires.

1. Identify your goals for connecting—looking for partners, advisors, allies, investors, mentors, participants, clients, benefactors, educators, influencers, team members, employers, employees, recipients, implementers. But be sure to leave yourself open to discovering reasons to connect that you may not have thought about before meeting. Curious serendipity, baby.
2. Curiously look for legitimate reasons to like people you wish to connect with. It is easier for you to actively find things you like about another person than to control whether that person likes you. Likability is a huge factor in the art and science of persuasion.[34]
3. Curiously look for ways to genuinely help them. When you're working to do good stuff in the world, start by doing good stuff for the person with whom you want to connect. Although reciprocity is a huge factor in the art and science of persuasion, do this as a gift with no expectation of reciprocity except to like the recipient more and feel more connected.[35]
4. Curiously look for ways to connect with people who can influence others. Your initial connections can provide social proof and authority, which help you

> gain more connections. It's more persuasive to have others sing your praises to support your cause than for you to sing your own.[36] This is especially true if you're a sucky singer, like me.

Sometimes we connect on things we have in common that we really like (or love); sometimes we connect on things we have in common that we dislike (or hate). Both are powerful connectors. Don't worry about the intensity and sacredness of the word *love*. The purpose is to find things that inspire a similar positive emotion or reaction in both of you. Likewise, don't worry about the negativity of the word *hate*. It doesn't have to be something that you both actually hate, but it should be things that create a similar negative emotion or reaction in both of you. Here are some common areas to look for commonalities.

Common Areas to Look for Commonalities...and Some Uncommon Examples

- Family dynamics (for example, you were both raised by your immigrant grandfathers)
- Friend dynamics (for example, you both have a best friend who won Mr. Universe)
- Jobs (for example, you both worked as law clerks on a big case that had been all over the news)
- Goals (for example, you both want to work to combat racism in America)
- Places of study (for example, you both studied for major exams in a cemetery)
- Areas of study (for example, you both studied the molecular biology of mollusks)
- Travel (for example, you both spent a year living in Turkey)
- Geography (for example, you are both from the same tiny village in China)
- Health (for example, you both have a hereditary autoimmune disease)

- Business (for example, you both have had two unsuccessful franchise experiences)
- Careers (for example, you both have law degrees but have been out of the work force for fifteen years while raising kids)
- Hobbies (for example, you both feel insect photography is superior to meditation for relaxation)
- Sports (for example, you both competed for an Olympic spot in swimming)
- Experiences (for example, you both had a near-death experience while skiing)
- Humor (for example, you both love obscure British comedy)
- Entertainment (for example, you both hate *Star Wars*)
- Food (for example, you both like spicy grasshoppers in mole sauce)
- Animals (for example, you have both been bitten by a venomous snake)
- Books (for example, you both love Kurt Vonnegut)
- Movies (for example, you both cry every time you watch *Rocky*)
- History (for example, you both have been wrongly imprisoned for more than a year)
- Music (for example, you both love old Appalachian love songs)
- Science (for example, you both aced organic chemistry… after failing it the first time)
- Television (for example, you were both best friends with a popular childhood actor)
- Philanthropy (for example, you were both in the Peace Corps in Cambodia)
- Medical (for example, you both have ex-husbands who have undergone more than four cosmetic plastic surgeries)
- Successes (for example, you both won a Poetry Slam competition)
- Dental (for example, you both had front teeth knocked out by a sibling)
- Past (for example, you both considered priesthood)

Exercise 4.2: Connect with Love and Hate

Finding the uncommon commonalities takes investigation. Here's how to do it.

1. Write down the names of 5 people you would like to connect with. These folks should relate to a goal or project you have. Feel free to start with a tiny project to test it first. Ideally, some of these people would have the ability to refer you to other people that you can involve in this project and in future projects too. It's great if some people on your list relate directly to your goal—what I call matchers—and some can introduce you to those matchers—what I call matchmakers.

2. Conduct research on each of these people. No, this is not stalking, silly. Your intent is to curiously look for ways to connect in order to do your good stuff. Look on social media; read articles, interviews, and websites; ask your friends and acquaintances who might know them; or ask the people directly if you can interview them for your Living Curiously project. Here are some slightly unusual ideas for you to investigate or ask about:

   - What are they most proud of?
   - What did their childhood smell like?
   - What book or advice would they give to their younger self?
   - If they could have a billboard with any message, where would they put it and what would the message be?
   - What specific thing do they hope to accomplish before they're ninety years old?
   - What allergy, illness, or tragedy have they suffered?
   - Do they have a silly, unusual skill?
   - Whom do they most admire?
   - What embarrasses them?

- What makes them laugh?
- What's the biggest way they have changed since they were six?
- What surprised them most?
- What bothers them?
- What's their least favorite food?
- What's their favorite type of music?
- What would they be happy knowing that you learned about them?

3. As you look over the things you identified about each person, genuinely match things that you both *love* (or really like). For example, perhaps you are both huge fans of the local sports team. Great, that's a love connection, but it may not qualify as uncommon unless it's an obscure team like the Muckdogs from Batavia, New York (and you live in Hillsboro, Oregon), or an obscure sport like ga-ga ball (which I played a lot as a kid at summer camp) or extreme ironing (which I'm kind of intrigued to try). If you both share an interest in a particular player that is not the agreed-upon star, maybe that's a love connection that is a little less common. If that player came from a team overseas that you both followed, that could be a love connection of a more uncommon variety.

4. Now genuinely match things you both *hate* (or really dislike). Filling in the following blanks can help:
   - Even though most people don't find _____ very _____, that is one thing that creates a negative emotion for me.
   - Most people wouldn't care about_____ but I think that (name)_____ would care because, like me, they also _____.

5. To create opportunities for reciprocity, fill in the blanks below:
   - I can make (name)_____'s life better by _____.

- (name)_____ can make my life better by _____ because then we can both _____.

Out of your love and hate commonalities, identify the most meaningful uncommon commonality you can find. It doesn't have to be wildly uncommon. I was once hired to speak at a conference because of an initial connection resulting from an uncommon dislike for chocolate. It may have helped that several people were chastising the person who hired me for not liking chocolate, and I honestly chimed in that I too find chocolate way overrated.

What would make you most curious if someone were to find an uncommon commonality with you? What would make you say, "I cannot believe the coincidence"? Go look for that. The magic is that the commonality will provide the connection even if it's unrelated to your vision or efforts in ethical persuasion.

6. Practice this with a couple people you know fairly well before connecting with the people on your list that you don't know as well.

Contact some friends or comfortable acquaintances and share your genuine discovery of uncommon commonalities with them. People you know well will find this fun—like a new discovery. Then see what happens when you invite them to be your guest to something related to your uncommon commonality, or send them an interesting article based on your uncommon commonality, or find something beneficial to do for them. Share your goal and ask them to get involved or make an introduction to someone who might want to get involved.

7. Now try this with the people on your list from number 1.

Connecting should not be or feel fake or disingenuous. Let your curiosity go wild. If you're curious enough, most people are interesting. If you're not curious about some people, they are probably not the right people to connect with. Keep looking. If you have already contacted at least one person from your list, you just racked up six more bonus points. If not, give yourself at least two bonus points for making it through Step 4.

Quick Q & A

It takes finesse to use uncommon commonalities well and make those connections. Here are some commonly asked questions and helpful answers so you can connect with confidence.

When is the best time to mention uncommon commonalities?

It's best to strategically reveal the uncommon commonality at the beginning of your interaction. The persuasive and connecting power of similarity will be the filter through which the rest of your communication flows.

When can uncommon commonalities cause the achievement of my goal to unravel?

If you're not really looking to arouse the buy curious, this strategy will not work. If you are not really curious, this exercise will be seen as manipulative instead of exciting and connecting. If you fail to pay attention to the persuasive power of reciprocity and fail to learn what you can do to benefit the person with whom you're trying to connect, you will be seen as pushy and self-serving. You must be deserving of the help you seek.

What can I do to amplify the power of finding uncommon commonalities?

Look for legitimate opportunities to compliment and elevate others. Don't wait to see what they can do for you before you look for ways to do something for them. If they acknowledge your help, *let them know that you especially love to help people who share <insert uncommon commonality here>—that's what you people who <insert uncommon commonality here> do for one another.*

What if every time the Living Curiously Method suggested that I write or draw something, I didn't actually take the action? What if I just did it as a mental exercise?

It will certainly help you to think about the steps of the Living Curiously Method, but it may not work as well if you just think about them. Infuse your goals with the memory-enhancing power of visual (picture), acoustic (sound), and semantic (meaning). Even if you're not an artist (and perhaps especially if you're not an artist), drawing taps into parts of the brain that thinking alone does not. Plus, when you write down your goals, they are more persuasive because commitments you make actively (in writing, drawing, or out loud in front of witnesses) stick around longer.[37] Besides, you can't give yourself maximum bonus points if you don't do the work.

What exactly am I selling?

Doing good stuff involves creating and inspiring beneficial change. This probably means that you're addressing a problem, or at least something that is less than optimal. Start with making the problem clear. Then arouse curiosity in your inspiration, ideas, mission, service, technology, product, or vision—your solution and contribution to the wheelwork of the universe.

" *Every living being is an engine geared to the wheelwork of the universe. Though seemingly affected only by its immediate surrounding, the sphere of external influence extends to infinite distance.* —NIKOLA TESLA

Spread your ideas because, as Seth Godin put it, "Ideas that spread, win."

Step 5: BLAST: Blunder, Learn, Accumulate Successes, Try (Again)

❝ *Life is either a daring adventure or nothing at all.*
—Helen Keller

❝ *Life is trying things to see if they work.* —Ray Bradbury

Now that you've created a perfect vision—and have done Steps 1 through 4 to prep it—it's time to take imperfect action. Imperfect action trumps perfect stagnation. Step 5 shows you how to do this, broken down into four stages. The stages should take you from laptop to liftoff. They make up the handy acronym BLAST:

1. Blunder
2. Learn
3. Accumulate Successes
4. Try (again)

Key Benefits

There are four key benefits to BLASTing:

- Reframing failure
- Revealing hidden successes
- Understanding the innovate-execute conundrum
- Understanding the quit-fail conundrum

To understand all this failure-versus-success talk and BLAST's benefits, first we need to look at the fear of failure.

Fear of Failure—A Tricky Pest

Most of us have experienced how the fear of failure can be paralyzing, stopping us from taking action. On the other end of the spectrum, this fear is also a powerful motivator to take the type of action that can skew our judgment and limit our successes. What? Fear both paralyzes us *and* causes us to act in a less-than-optimal way? Yep. Research shows us that fear stops us from taking action (we knew that, right?). But research also shows that fear is the driving force that motivates us to take action to avoid pain (failure) more often than it is the force that motivates us to seek pleasure (success). This follows in line with loss-aversion research, which suggests that we strongly prefer avoiding loss to acquiring gain.[38]

Awareness of this judgment trap may lessen its effect, but go ahead and test it on yourself with this A/B test. Now that you're aware of this force, which of these headlines would entice you to read further?

A. 5 Ways that Your Computer History Says You're Healthy
B. 5 Ways that Your Computer History Says You're Going to Die

A. 7 Tips for Looking Smart in the Media
B. 7 Tips for Avoiding Looking Like an Idiot in the Media

A. 5 Ways to Avoid Having a Paper Cut Get You Fired!
B. 5 Ways to Use a Paper Cut to Get Your Perfect Job!

A. The 6 Best Steps to Avoid Total Failure

B. The 6 Best Steps for Total Success

(Give yourself eight bonus points if you're willing to conduct this A/B test by writing and publishing blog content for any of these headlines).

There are no right answers, but if you're like many unconventional thinkers, you may be more inclined to grab for success than worry about failure...or you're skeptical of whether you'd take the time to read any of the proffered headlines. It's all good. Reach around your own neck and give yourself a free massage for choosing A or B anyway...and for not allowing fear to direct you away from success.

Reframing Failure

Failure feels most right when we see it in the rearview mirror while we're steering securely on the road to success. Let's face it, people in the middle of failure rarely get big book deals or guest spots on talk shows unless they're donning electronic ankle bracelets. Those deals come after big failures are firmly in the past. And people don't tend to talk about their failures until they're safely behind too—because at that point, the success is the focal point. We can point to our heroes and say, "Yeah, I'm failing just like he did." The unspoken hope that follows is, "Therefore, I will succeed just like he did." But how do we know others' failure-success paths will be related to our own?

Does having a past failure in common mean having a future success in common? If not, how do we achieve insights that will help us discover the difference between those who fail and ultimately are deemed unremarkable, and those who fail and ultimately *are* deemed remarkable? It's hard because, while we do have case studies and books about spectacular failures, we rarely hear about endeavors that have failed in obscurity. We actually have limited understanding of the lessons of failure. Curiosity provides those lessons.

In addition to the fear, avoidance, and limited understanding of failure, there is the convenient problem of justifying mistakes.

This can stand in the way of learning from them. In response to this, a whole industry has crept up about the benefits and power of failure. Marketers promise to teach you how to fail well, fail fast, fail forward, fail sideways so you'll ultimately succeed. Welcome failure and you shall prosper, they say. But is this remarkable? Is this living curiously?

The Living Curiously Method suggests viewing failure with curiosity instead of welcoming arms or cold shoulders. This allows us to question whether there are common threads in failure and mistake stories that are also the common threads in the inspirational success stories. Curiosity reveals hidden insights that may be more positively correlated with success. The trend to embrace failure is certainly comforting, but deep in the recesses of our minds, we know that rewards don't come to those who fail—at least not until after a subsequent success when the failures can become part of the inspiring narrative. What if curiosity allowed us to reframe failure to become more like an instructive blunder than a useless mistake?

The old way: Overcome Fear of Failure → Success
The new way: Blunder, Learn, Accumulate Successes, Try again (BLAST)

Revealing Hidden Successes
When you peek intentionally, you'll find that hidden in the debris of every blunder are pieces of success waiting to be discovered. These successes may or may not fit with your current vision of the puzzle you're trying to put together for your life, but find and accumulate them anyway. They will be useful.

Let's say you wrote a book about how to get insurance companies to pay when they don't want to pay. You felt like a failure because of your unsuccessful attempt to crowdfund the publication of your book. You barely raised any money. Because of the failed crowdfunding campaign, you thought your book concept was a bust.

But you were wise and undefeated. You dug around curiously and became aware of an urgent philanthropic crowdfunding campaign to house families whose homes were destroyed in a huge landslide. This crowdfunding campaign was sucking resources from your exact target audience. Is this a hint as to why your crowdfunding endeavor may not have achieved the funding goal? You also found an online forum where people who were supporting this philanthropic endeavor were looking for some way to help these families navigate insurance claims. Your project was referenced. Sweet success! Now you have found an audience and a specific cause. Had you dismissed your campaign without curiosity, you may have missed the opportunity to benefit people by finding a different way (or different timing) to get your helpful information out.

Elevate curiosity because, although your accomplishment may fall short, long, or sideways relative to what you were trying to accomplish, those successes accumulating on the side can become part of a different and perhaps more remarkable puzzle.

Also, how often are we so seduced by accomplishment that we fail to see the turn-on of potential? Potential is unrealized possibility, and it ties in seamlessly with BLASTing.

Blunder

So the first stage of the final step of the Living Curiously Method is to blunder. Failure and success share a continuum, with failure perched on the opposite end from success. A blunder can be somewhere in between. Perhaps that's why failure has a sense of finality that a blunder does not. A blunder is less scary.

The Living Curiously Method doesn't just propose overcoming your fear of failure; it also proposes actively seeking opportunities to blunder toward your goals. Simple semantics? Maybe. But sometimes when something like the mantra "Overcome your fear of failure!" becomes a common platitude, we stop being curious about how to actually do it. So blunder instead.

Exercise 5.1: Blunder Like a Beginner
Blundering is really not that hard or scary. Here's how to start getting comfortable with blundering.

1. Select at least 3 of the following projects and commit to taking imperfect action.

- Write your bio as you want it to appear in some public way in a year.
- Make business cards with your dream title. Mark your calendar for when you will pass them out.
- Volunteer to speak for free on your area of expertise at a nursing home.
- Publicly state your specific plan to do good stuff.
- Quit your job and do something better.
- Start to write a book and tell people when you'll publish it.
- Invite friends and neighbors to participate in a focus group for your idea.
- Book a trip to research your idea.
- Join an organization and run or volunteer for a leadership role within the organization.
- Publicly offer to provide consulting or coaching services.
- Record a video of your vision. Post it somewhere public.
- Pick one societal problem, research solutions from opposing groups, and meet with a leader to discuss your findings.
- Publicly change your mind about an important topic.
- Register your business and write your business plan.
- Try out for a role, team, or group.
- Ask for a promotion.
- Put on some kind of performance.
- Make a public declaration of loving someone or something.
- Write up your proposal and give it to your boss.
- Create something and share it with 5 people.
- Try something you've never done before and teach 3 people how to do it.

- Create a website and send the link to 5 people.
- Take the first significant leap beyond what is blocking you from your goal.
2. Identify 2 ways that each of your chosen projects could be blunders.
3. Identify 2 successes that could result from each of your chosen projects.
4. Identify 2 ways each chosen project could be both a blunder *and* a success.

Blunder Assessment

Let's say you take on an audaciously big project to do good stuff—like eradicating hunger in the next fifteen years. What if it actually takes nineteen years to accomplish your mission? Would that be a blunder or a success or both? You might be thinking, *That's ridiculous to consider that achievement to be a blunder at all when the accomplishment is so incredibly profound. That's a success!* In many ways you would be correct. However, if you had given your goal only one extra year (sixteen years) instead of four extra years (nineteen years), the assessment could have been very different. Blunders contain successes, and successes contain blunders. In this example, perhaps the blunder was being enticed by easy, round numbers (like fifteen years) for goal setting when curious consideration of a different or more precise analysis may have provided a better time frame.

While the thumb on the scale of measurement is often time, similar addiction to round-number goal setting has made a billion dollars a rounding error. Huge undertakings make more precise goal setting difficult. History showcases this only too well. Here is one of history's stories.

Can Space Success Be Achieved in Spite of Spacey Budgets?

The space race was on and the Cold War was...heating up? On May 25, 1961, President John F. Kennedy stood before a special session of Congress and announced that the United States would send an American safely to the Moon (and back) before the end of the decade. The initial plan was to make the goal 1967, the fiftieth anniversary of the Bolshevik Revolution.[39] Coincidence? Kennedy expected the Apollo program to cost $531 million in 1962 and an additional $7 to $9 billion dollars over the following five-year period, for a total of under 10 billion dollars.

On July 20, 1969 (not a year too soon), astronauts Neil Armstrong and Buzz Aldrin, of the *Apollo 11* mission, landed the Lunar Module on the surface of the Moon. Four days later they landed safely back on Earth.[40]

Mission accomplished? It depends on how you look at it. In 1967, when a fire in the cabin of *Apollo 1* killed the entire crew during a prelaunch test, many deemed the mission a failure. If there was strict budgetary accountability, the mission wasn't successful because the Apollo program went billions over budget. The program ultimately cost over $24 billion (over $100 billion in today's dollars). Were the billions of dollars over Kennedy's 1961 estimate just a rounding error back then? Probably not. The creation of the initial spending budget was certainly a blunder...or a very unlucky guess.[41]

There are, however, tremendous successes from Apollo that reach far beyond the Cold War tit for tat and carry on in our lives today. It's not easy to assess the ultimate value of the remarkable products that spun off from the Apollo program[42] because we are still reaping benefits. In addition to great advancements in civil, mechanical, and electrical engineering, we can credit the program for giving us flame-resistant clothing, freeze-dried food, thirst-quenching Tang, water purification systems, and kidney dialysis machines, among many other useful products. Most Americans agree that the mission to land on the Moon was ultimately a success, despite the blunders. See the difference?

"
It's clearly a budget. It's got a lot of numbers.
—GEORGE W. BUSH

The timing of measuring and assessing your successes matters. The political and scientific justifications for the space race were and are vast, relevant, and worthy of curious consideration in the assessment of successes. However, these justifications should not trump curiosity about blunders of budgets, time frames, and decisions. Elevating curiosity reveals lessons we can learn and use to accomplish big, audacious goals in the future.

> **"** *I have not failed. I've just found 10,000 ways that won't work.* —THOMAS EDISON

Learn

The difference between a wasteful failure and a useful blunder lies in the ability to learn from the experience. The goal is not only to learn from your blunders but also to think more insightfully about the key things *to* learn.

Reflection

Exercise 5.2: Learn from Your Blunders
You can start noticing the valuable lessons from your blunder early on. Here's how.

1. When a project appears to be a blunder, write down your initial assumption about why it did not work.
2. Write down 4 alternative possible reasons and 4 preposterous reasons for the blunder.
3. Write down 2 justifications.
4. Look for blunders similar to your own in different industries, cultures, and situations. Could any of the reasons for these blunders apply to you?
5. What would need to happen for you to abandon your goal?
6. Remember that time is tricky. Are you assessing your results too late? Are you assessing too soon?
7. Predict what would happen if you changed 1 specific thing, 2 specific things, or 3 specific things.
8. What are 3 ways you can assess the blunder differently?

The clearer and more precise your mission, the easier it is to measure your outcomes against how you're doing.

" *Hey, how ya doin'?* —LITTLE MIX, RAPPER

And when you've accumulated some successes, it's even easier to see insightful and plentiful lessons learned from blunders.

Accumulate Successes

As mentioned, measuring your outcomes and appropriately appreciating your blunders doesn't always mean that the successes will be obvious. It isn't always easy to find successes, nor is it always easy to differentiate useful successes from justifications—that's where your curiosity comes in. The more audacious your mission, the more opportunities you'll have to blunder and the more piles of debris you'll have to go through to curiously excavate hidden successes.

When you blunder to learn your way toward your goals, it is not only necessary to gather successes, but it is also critical to heed the lessons provided along the way. Oh, they are there, but because successes are often hidden with the lessons like crumbs in a couch, you have to be curious enough to move the cushions. When we jump from curiosity to criticism or judgment too quickly, we often miss the opportunity to accumulate successes in order to learn from them. Identifying successes will be easier for you than other people because you're using the Living Curiously Method and you started with what you're not. Let me explain. Success will include the wrong people rejecting the pursuit of your goals for the right reasons, and you'll know this because you've identified who your audience is and isn't. Success will include the illumination of insights—like when rejection means you're on the right track.

We miss educational successes when we quickly identify reasons for complete failure without curiosity. Accumulating these successes requires elevating curiosity when we're analyzing both our own blunders and the blunders of others. Apple Inc. and the band U2 provide an example of how even admired companies and beloved music groups can blunder...and how we miss the successes when we're too quick to judge. Here is their story.

Is There a Winning Loophole in a Losing Freebie?

Thanks but no thanks—that was the response. In 2014, Apple decided to award 500 million iTunes users with a free automatic install of the Irish band U2's newest album, *Songs of Innocence*. Apple, analysts, and U2 thought the decision would be celebrated as a brilliant business move and a generous gift from a most beloved American company and the world's most popular Irish band. They were wrong.

When U2 haters and other annoyed recipients took to social media to voice their frustration and disdain, Apple was surprised. The company had to madly scramble to provide a special button—and a dedicated webpage with step-by-step instructions—to allow users to delete the album from their accounts. The generous gift was consistently described as a public relations disaster—a failure.

Immediately after the Apple-U2 project was deemed a big failure, naysayers entered the typical mad rush to show off their authority. They quickly identified the mistakes that caused the failure. Their reasons were as emphatically stated as they were varied:

- Apple failed to understand that U2 was past its prime. (Industry insiders called U2 a "dad band.") The assumption was that this would have worked with cooler artists.
- You can't treat music like spam, or people will rebel. The assumption was that you can't blatantly force stuff on customers—it's creepy.
- Apple is cool, but its coolness doesn't extend beyond technology and into what's cool to listen to. The assumption was that Apple overstepped its area of expertise.
- Apple superstar events are over. The assumption was that Apple should refrain from doing superstar events in the future.
- Downloads are passé. The assumption was that a streaming option would have been applauded.

- The Apple and U2 connection is too elite, cozy, and insider. The assumption was that this would have worked with a less mainstream company or band.
- Consumers prefer to earn their freebies rather than have freebies pushed at them without their consent. The assumption was that the content didn't matter, but the problem was how the content was provided.
- Giving away music for free devalues all music. The assumption was that people didn't value the U2 album because it was free.

Analyses like these were all over the media and blogosphere. History was written. Many read the analyses with knowing smirks, relishing the fact that even cherished giants can fail. Reading articles and blog posts, people following the hoopla chose the reason for the failure they most agreed with, and most of us looked no further. Perhaps it's true that the Apple-U2 project was a public relations blunder; however, a curious search beyond the obvious reveals hidden successes.

Statistically, the 38 million people who accessed the album tallied up to far more than would have bought or heard it normally. Maybe the real reason most analysts didn't see how this project was more successful than the seemingly obvious failure indicated was because some of the success was more complicated. Our fast-paced news cycle often leaves little time for the strategic curiosity necessary to uncover the successes that can provide important lessons, and this was no different.

No small part of the success of the Apple-U2 love affair had to do with a complicated tax loophole with a cute jump-ropey name of "Double Irish."[43] It was a special tax arrangement in Ireland, one that U2's Bono was an outspoken proponent of, and one that Apple legally used to its huge tax-saving advantage. Essentially, using the Double Irish resulted in a huge tax savings. It allowed companies like Apple to transfer royalty payments for intellectual property to a firm in Ireland and onto an Irish-registered subsidiary in a country with no corporate income tax. There was also the "Dutch Sandwich," which was an even more intricate tax loophole.[44] This one allowed the transfer between two Irish firms to be routed to the Netherlands to further reduce the amount of tax paid. U2 enjoyed this Dutch Sandwich in 2006, when they moved the company that handles their publishing royalties from Ireland to the Netherlands. Could it be that the opportunity to take advantage of these tax loopholes had a role in Apple pairing up with U2 for the giveaway?

Taking advantage of legal tax loopholes may not seem like a positive reason to label any part of the Apple-U2 venture a success, but if you were an Apple shareholder, an Irish government employee, or a recipient of Bono's enormous efforts to fight AIDS and poverty, you might feel differently. If not, curiously looking for successes may help us see how trying the same type of corporation-band partnership with a hipper band, for example, could be costly in other ways.

" *First the doctor told me the good news: I was going to have a disease named after me.* —Steve Martin

Exercise 5.3: Shift into Success Mode

After you've analyzed your blunders and learned from them, it's time to shift into success mode.

1. Identify the 3 least important good things that happened this week.
2. Identify 3 people to contact to give them a sincere compliment about their efforts to be remarkable and do good stuff.
3. Compliment yourself about 3 things you did right last month in your efforts to be remarkable and do good stuff.
4. Identify 1 thing that you did—or something that happened—to move you toward your goal.

When we reframe less-than-ideal outcomes as blunders and strategically apply curiosity, we learn lessons and reveal accumulated successes. It's not always enough to just focus on why an effort supposedly failed. I know evaluating blunders is hard enough when they happen to other people, let alone when they happen to us. So focus on accumulating successes, and that will maximize your valuable lessons to apply as you move forward.

Try (Again)

" *Kids, you tried your best and you failed miserably. The lesson is, never try.* —HOMER SIMPSON

After you have blundered, learned, and accumulated successes, BLASTing involves *trying again*. It is the way to test your insights, judgments, and decisions. BLASTing is a cycle of incorporating life, adventure, and work insights into the Living Curiously Method and going after your goals.

" *The way through the challenge is to get still and ask yourself, 'What is the next right move? What is the next right move?' and then, from that space, make the next right move and the next right move.* —OPRAH WINFREY

Within the framework of BLASTing, trying again will provide unfamiliar fresh perspectives. Trying again requires embracing the unfamiliar and the uncertain. Uncertainty gets short-sheeted because fear gets in the way of understanding how glorious uncertainty can be. Uncertainty fuels curiosity at the same time that replacing fear with curiosity fuels uncertainty. It's a beautiful, symbiotic relationship.

" *There are things known and there are things unknown, and in between are the doors of perception.* —ALDOUS HUXLEY

Trying again increases your chances of serendipitous encounters. Those encounters not only provoke insights, but they also

increase your chances of discovering adventure that inspires...
and they're fun!

Exercise 5.4: Prepare to Try Again

As with all difficult tasks, trying again is made easier with preparation.

1. Choose 3 things to do from the list below:
   - Pick 3 new ways to look at something you pass every day.
   - Novelty is everywhere and always. Think of all the things that changed in the few seconds between reading the first part of this sentence and the last. Write down 3 ways that *this* very second is different from *this* very second.
   - If you could hold on to one memory for all eternity, what would it be?
   - Pick something you dislike doing and write down 3 novel features of the task.
   - If you were to schedule time in each day for novelty, how much time would you allot?
   - Write a letter to your future self. Hide it in a book. Create a reminder to yourself to dig it out.
2. Identify 3 things that you should try again.
3. For each of those, identify 3 ways that you will try it again...differently.

To BLAST effectively, it's important to acknowledge and re-spect two pesky conundrums. Conundrums are like riddles or puzzling questions. A question like, "Why do psychics still have to work if they all know the winning lottery numbers?" could be a type of conundrum. Another conundrum is whether you have achieved success or failure if you try to fail and succeed. But those aren't exactly the types of conundrums I'm talking about when it comes to BLASTing.

Key Benefits

Taking the kind of imperfect action required when you BLAST means that you will come face-to-face with the innovate-execute conundrum and the quit-fail conundrum. Remember those from the list of key benefits for this step of the Method? I knew you were paying attention!

In the first conundrum, moving toward a goal requires understanding when to innovate (think, learn, test, assess, etc.), and when to execute (launch, go, try, etc.). It isn't always clear when to primarily focus on one or the other because the Living Curiously Method involves both innovating and executing. It is critical to be aware of this tricky balance.

The quit-fail conundrum addresses the puzzling question of when *quitting* is failure and when *failure to quit* is failure. Not acknowledging these conundrums could leave you susceptible to missing hidden insights that can help steer you toward your goal.

Understanding the Innovate-Execute Conundrum

" *How wonderful that we have met with a paradox. Now we have some hope of making progress.* —NIELS BOHR

Too much innovation and not enough execution is like seeing without being—at best it's a mirage, and at worst it's a hallucination. However, execution without innovation is depletion. It sucks your work, your adventures, and your life dry. Therein lies the conundrum. Out of curiosity, what's the right balance?

The best visionaries are often not the best executers. This is true for both life and work experiences. In the life cycle of a company, there are ideal times for innovation and ideal times for execution. The same applies in our own lives. Often well-intended friends will tell you to just go for it when you're very well aware that you are still in researching-and-idea-generating mode. Your hesitancy to try again doesn't necessarily mean that you're afraid to launch or even that you're working toward an unachievable ideal of perfection. (However, if that is indeed the case, bust yourself.)

It may very well mean that you are appropriately innovating in preparation for executing.

When ideas are generating and snowballing like an avalanche in your brain, that's associative activation. Idea generation is fun and inspiring, but sometimes it results in errors. A damaging consequence of theses errors is that they can cause an innovation-spewing spinout that results in inaction. Do you have friends who have so many interesting ideas that they never act on any of them? Who, me? Okay, maybe they race out and secure the domain name, but they do little beyond that. They could have a bad case of associative activation.

> **"** *Genius is one percent inspiration and ninety-nine percent perspiration.* —THOMAS EDISON

Tom Edison was already forty-one years old when the first underarm deodorant, Mum, was developed and patented by a US inventor in Philadelphia. Perhaps that's why he attributed so much genius to perspiration. But is the right balance between perspiration (execution) and inspiration (innovation) really ninety-nine to one? I'm skeptical of this math.

For example, when we invest in learning about what makes great parenting, what fosters relationships, what attracts our mates, how to please our partners, or what inspiring visionaries do to create lives we admire, we need time to process the information. Only then can we begin to apply it meaningfully to our own lives.

But once we do, when is it better to continue to process and innovate, and when is it better to take action and execute? When is it better to stop planning the trip and fantasizing about how you're going to document your adventure, and when is it time to book your flight and go? These questions do not imply that there is always more value in executing than innovating. Innovating is a huge part of adventuring, learning, and even blundering. The innovate-execute conundrum is not necessarily an either-or, but rather a balance. Pay attention to this balance, and do not let fear of execution delay your decision to tilt from innovation mode to execution mode.

If your adventure or do-good project involves building a tribe or team, there will be some folks who are better executers and others who are better innovators. Decisions about who should lead the team depend on where you are in the cycle of your project or business. You should be aware that the time to shift from innovation to execution and back is not always obvious to a leader who favors one mode versus another. It is critical to infuse your team with innovation-strong *and* execution-strong folks so you create the right balance.

If you find yourself stuck in idea mode, at some point it will be time to go from laptop to liftoff. When you're stuck in execute mode, at some point it's important to retreat, recharge, and innovate. There is no magic answer to achieve the perfect balance—that's why it's a conundrum—but it's best to be aware of and remain curious about its existence and about the best way to balance the conundrum.

Understanding the Quit-Fail Conundrum

The fourth key benefit to BLASTing is understanding the quit-fail conundrum. When is quitting a bigger blunder than failing to quit? When you're stuck, trapped in a cycle of self-doubt, excitement, anxiety, encouragement, and discouragement about the future, this conundrum pops up like Whac-a-Mole at the arcade.

"*Winners never quit and quitters never win.*
—Vince Lombardi

(If you take more than 5 minutes disproving this common statement, please quit something.)

"*Quitting is the easiest thing to do.* —Robert Kiyosaki

(Really? Tell that to a smoker...or me with just a few more chips left in the bowl and half a margarita in my glass.)

Important Quit-Fail Conundrum Considerations

There are two important considerations when it comes to the quit-fail conundrum: sunk costs and opportunity costs. Sunk costs are about the past. These costs include time, money, and mental and emotional energy spent in the past as a result of a past decision. Whether the outcome is good, bad, or not yet determined, these costs are sunk because they are impossible to recover. Although we can't get these costs back, we still often give them far too much consideration when we're deciding where we are on the quit-fail spectrum.

Have you ever gone to the theater, paid way too much for a movie, and known in less than fifteen minutes that it was not good? Come on, not even *Gigli* or *Conan the Barbarian*? If you stayed to watch the rest of the movie and a tiny bit of the reason you stayed was because you paid so much for the movie, you were trapped in the sunk-cost quicksand. Failure to quit is too often the result of focusing too much on sunk costs.

I often used to see clients focusing heavily on sunk costs in my real estate career. Irrespective of mortgage loans and balances, sellers would often use what they paid for their property and the costs for improvements, upgrades, and remodeling when determining their sale price. They failed to see that whether they got those improvements free as a gift from their brother the builder or paid top retail dollar was irrelevant. Buyers rarely care about those things when considering what to pay. What one initially pays and what one spends on improvements are sunk costs.

The other side of that, and the second important consideration of the conundrum, is that opportunity costs are about the future. They are the immediate costs of not taking the next best alternative. When we don't consider quitting as an option, for example, we fail to assess opportunity costs. In the movie example, if we fail to value what we could enjoy if we bailed on the bad movie to do something more fun, we fail to analyze our opportunity cost. Our opportunity cost might be seeing a different great movie, going dancing, or getting a late-night workout. In the real estate example, if we focus on trying to recover all of the remodeling costs, we fail to examine our opportunity costs like the next place we miss out on buying while we wait to sell an overpriced house. When we're assessing whether quitting is a bigger blunder than failing to quit, it is critical to understand these concepts of sunk costs and opportunity costs.

Sunk costs → the past
Opportunity costs → the future

The next tricky layer to this conundrum is that when we *do* consider quitting as an option, we often create fallback options. These fallback options can make quitting too soon a tiny bit more likely.[45] I know that this is exhausting, but being curious about this conundrum will help you make better decisions. Here's one way it helped me.

Leaving my lucrative career in real estate was my own big quitting experience. Quitting was not easy because my career was long, fruitful, and fun. There were opportunity costs associated with quitting, like the consistently good income from real estate and consistently interesting real estate clients. There were opportunity costs associated with not quitting, like fully embracing and writing *Living Curiously* and sharing the Living Curiously Method. It wasn't always easy to push the sunk costs—the years and money spent building my business—from my mind, but I would never get those back, whether I quit or stayed. When I weighed them out as strategically as I was able, the opportunity costs of not quitting were far too great.

If you're curious enough to look, sunk costs are clear. They're spent. Opportunity costs take more guessing. It's hard to assess whether protecting and potentially adding more sunk costs gets you closer to success, or whether it's best to move on and bury the sunk costs to avoid higher opportunity costs.[46]

Exercise 5.5: Ask Yourself
To try to evaluate sunk costs and opportunity costs, and where you are on the quit-fail spectrum, ask yourself these questions. Don't worry about coming up with concrete

Reflection

answers to all of these questions, but do skim them and give them each 7 seconds of thought. Seven seconds will be good luck for your curiosity, and these questions will come in handy in all kinds of situations.

- Are my goals realistic?
- Am I realistically assessing the odds of success?
- Am I relying too heavily on positive thinking? Not enough?
- Am I relying on too few examples of similar successes?
- Specifically why do I think I can defy the odds?
- Am I paying enough attention to competition? Too much?
- Do I like movies about gladiators or is it just the sandals I like? (Just checking to make sure you're paying attention.)
- Am I accurately analyzing why others have failed? Succeeded?
- Do I have a pattern of quitting to watch out for?
- What are the costs of quitting? How many of those are sunk costs?
- What are the costs of not quitting?
- Have I created markers to encourage me to assess opportunity costs?
- How does the quit-fail conundrum affect my analysis along the way?
- Can I tweak my goals without quitting? Should I?
- What if success is just one more try away?
- What if success is just one more quit away?
- What does thoughtful quitting look like if I never consider quitting?
- What role does justification play in my analysis?
- What does inaction decide for me?
- Have I already achieved my goals? How do I know?
- How can I judge myself more compassionately and still be a more insightful quitter?

Remember, when you replace the word *failure* with *blunder*, analyzing quitting may be easier. Elevate curiosity to see if there are options that hide between quitting and persisting—there could be many options between a) persisting and b) quitting.

1. Old scenario:

    A. Persist
    B. Quit

2. New scenario:

    A. Persist
    B. Try again by doing the same things differently
    C. Try again by doing similar things differently
    D. Try again by doing different things the same way
    F. Try again by doing different things differently
    E. Quit

I'm not sure about Thomas Edison's ninety-nine to one recipe for genius, but the Living Curiously Method involves lots of inspiration, preparation, inspired action, and perspiration.

What do you have planned for your life? Exist? Or live large? Live perfectly imperfectly? The Method is not guaranteed to make all of your wildest dreams come true, but it is guaranteed to make your life more insightful and adventure filled. Followed diligently and with curiosity, it is absolutely guaranteed to help you be remarkable and do good stuff. Cue your favorite music, because now it's time for you to put the Method into action.

Part IV: Toolkit for Takeoff

D on't tell anybody, but you just earned sixteen more bonus points for sticking this landing and being curious enough to stay around for the after-party. You won.

Living curiously isn't easy, but by now I hope you think it will be worth it to create your remarkable life and to do the good stuff that you need to do—that the world needs you to do. You know it takes elevating curiosity and using curiosity hacks to help when it's especially hard. You see how following the five steps of the Living Curiously Method will help you make it happen. You've made amazing progress, and now it will be much easier to embrace the lifelong practice of continuing to identify what you're not, dumpster-diving your life, cross-pollinating, finding uncommon commonalities, and BLASTing. You've learned many tools along the way, and before you close these pages, I want to give you some additional tools that you can come back to when you need a little nudge toward curiosity or when you need help defining your goals for doing good stuff.

Trigger Tools
Remember the triggers for elevating curiosity? Triggers stimulate responses. Triggers cause behavior, thoughts, events, and situations to happen. There are common psychological triggers to which many of us react. For example, do you know that slightly guilty feeling that creeps in when you are given a free, tasty sample and then you don't buy what's being offered? Yep, that free sample is a trigger.

Triggers are personal; different things trigger different people to react differently. Trigger tools are handy when you create them for yourself to help you achieve your desired thought, behavior, or outcome.

> **❝***I call these anchors that you can connect to your tiny behavior. The key is to pick which routine is the right trigger for your small, simple behavior.*
> —B. J. Fogg, behavior design researcher

Throughout your journey with the Living Curiously Method, there will be personal triggers for you. You may have already encountered some. The main trigger to establish is the one that will help you elevate curiosity. Pick something—an imaginary switch, a teeter-totter, a snap of your fingers—to act as your trigger. As I shared earlier, one of my weird triggers is to conjure up the image of a pogo stick. Perhaps because a pogo stick is still one of my favorite toys, this is what I think of when I need a trigger to elevate curiosity. Whatever triggers a reordering of curiosity for you will work.

Curiously examining the gaps between stimulus and response can help you identify your triggers. Stephen Covey, of *7 Habits of Highly Effective People* authorship, was profoundly affected by reading about the gap between stimulus and response. He explained it with, "I began to stand in that gap and to look outside at the stimuli." Perhaps trying his technique will help you replace triggers that block you (like when someone you admire gives you a doubting eyebrow and skeptical sneer and you want to retract the goals you shared) with trigger tools that help you move forward with curiosity and insight (like when you realize that they just had Botox, their face is kind of stuck like that, and it has nothing to do with you). Analyze your gaps and fill them with helpful trigger tools.

The next two exercises will put you on the path to filling your toolkit with some additional tools to trigger thoughts that bust through what can otherwise block you.

> **"***I don't like that man. I must get to know him better.***
> — ABRAHAM LINCOLN

Exercise 6.1: Play What If?

In this exercise, first conjure your mental trigger tool to remind you to elevate curiosity. Now play What If with each scenario presented.

A. A driver cuts you off in traffic. *What if...*
- She is racing to pick up a dangerously sick relative?
- She is an inconsiderate dill weed?
- He is on the verge of peeing his pants?
- He is stressed about hearing tragic news, and he didn't see you?
- She is late to her parole hearing?
- She was called in to perform emergency surgery?
- He is late to work?

B. A person asks you for money. *What if...*
- She looks like a dirty beggar?

- He is an acquaintance who once helped you get a job?
- She is raising funds for a homeless charity?
- He is wearing a suit and seems embarrassed to have forgotten his wallet?
- He is a friend who has made unfortunate life choices?
- She reminds you of you?
- He's a dear friend who was deviously scammed?
- She is fundraising at a civic gala?
- Everyone is watching?
- No one will know?

C. Your boss yells at you. *What if...*
- You screwed up?
- He is waiting for the results of a biopsy of a suspicious lump?
- She has never yelled at you before?
- She constantly finds fault with your excellent work?
- He treats everyone that way?
- He was just yelled at by his boss for something he did?
- She was just yelled at by her boss for something you did?
- His child is dying?
- She caused a terrible accident last night?

D. Someone breaks into your car. *What if...*
- It was to hide from a deranged terrorist?
- It was to get money for drugs?
- It was to steal something that belonged to them?
- It was to get money for saving someone's life?
- She had a gun to her head?
- You left it unlocked?
- He was old and suffering from dementia?
- He was abused and suffering from addiction?

- It was your own son or daughter?
- She was a repeat felon?
- It was to hide a present for you?

Exercise 6.2: Take the "Why Are You Here?" Test

Reflection

When you receive a potentially provocative text, email, or other electronically written communication, before you respond, elevate curiosity and see if the meaning could be interpreted differently by using this technique. Your one-day-older self might thank you. Keep this one in your toolkit of helpful triggers for future use too.

1. Imagine the written message you receive is "Why are you here?"
2. Consider how to interpret the message when the emphasis shifts to different words.
   - *Why* are you here?
   - Why *are* you here?
   - Why are *you* here?
   - Why are you *here*?

   Could the meaning be different than your initial interpretation?
3. Look up the thread of communication to see if your co-communicator could have made the same mistake about your communication. Is there any way they could have misinterpreted your meaning or vibe?
4. Write down the reason you chose the attitude that was implied with the communication you received. This may help: Because of _____, I think the person who sent me that email/text meant it to sound _____. If I was wrong, then _____.

This test can also help guide your communication techniques so your own messages are properly understood.

Goal-Setting Tools

The next two exercises will help you use curiosity to define your goals.

Reflection

Exercise 6.3: Mentally Play Metaphoric Golf

Use these questions as part of your BLAST journey. How is your project like this golf game? Can you see some of the Method embedded in this mental golf game?

1. What's my goal? I'm going to hit that dimpled, little ball in the hole.
2. Can I be more specific? I'm going to hit that sucker in the hole on the first hit.
3. Is this realistic? Probably not, because only one person has ever gotten a hole in one on this course. And I suck at golf.
4. What's a more realistic goal? A triple bogey.
5. Really? No, but I have little experience golfing, so I will study the course and aim for the hole.
6. Success will be measured by what? The number of strokes it takes me to get that ball in the hole.
7. Compared to what? Par…and birdies, bogeys, and eagles.
8. What am I using? A Callaway Big Bertha driver, with other clubs on standby. A cool golf outfit might help too.
9. How will I measure my outcome? I will see where the ball lands relative to the hole when I tee off. I will see if the humor I provide my good golfer friends is at a sufficient level.
10. How will I learn from my blunder? I will check to make sure I'm not swinging at a mushroom disguised as a ball, I will not hit against the wind, I will not ignore the sand traps, I will assess which club I need to get my next shot to land in the hole, I will not be frustrated by the people rushing me from behind, I will not use the golf club that is bent from fort-building with the kids…

11. How about trying again? I'm going to get closer and closer to the hole (and probably, as I putt, I will get farther before closer) until I get it in. And then I'll line up for the next hole.

Exercise 6.4: Close the Gap

The gap between inspiration and inspired action is where your remarkability will be revealed. Closing that gap is ultimately how you'll do good stuff.

1. Start by answering two curious questions:
   - Are you good at judging distances?
   - What is the distance between your reality and what you want out of your life?

   Use the metric system or your favorite system of measurement, but put a meaningful number on the distance.
2. Now publicly state your goals. This is one of the biggest incentives to take action. State your goals to close the gap between your reality and your desire to be remarkable and do good stuff.

Propulsion

I'm going to publicly state some of my own goals. Here goes:

- I am going to work every day of the rest of my life to find the mystique in the mundane (starting today).
- I am going to film training for the Living Curiously Method all over the world (starting on Tuesday).
- I am going to build the Living Curiously Method into a business that allows me to do the good stuff that I want to do in the world (already in progress).
- I am going to teach the Living Curiously Method to at least 5,409 people who want to be remarkable and do good stuff (if you just read this, we're on our way).

- I am going to work with fun, interesting people to laugh, adventure, learn, and provoke myself and other people to design Living Curiously Lifestyles (already in progress).

Here's a cool opportunity for you to take the 30-Day Living Curiously Challenge for free. Go to www.LivingCuriously.net /30DayChallenge. You'll apply what you've learned in this book and be propelled toward inspired action.

The growing Tribe of the Curious sends a hearty cheers to you with a reminder of your invitation to join. We will be continuing to launch exciting opportunities to enhance your Living Curiously Lifestyle. Join for free at www.BeckiSaltzman.com/join-the-tribe -of-the-curious..

Exercise 6.5: Bonus Round*
Remember way back when you started with what you're not? Here's that bonus round I promised you at the end of Exercise 1.3.

1. Go back and grab your answers from Exercise 1.2: Get to Know Yourself.
2. Add up all the letters of your answers: A=1, B=2, C=3, and D=4, and try to discover the patterns.
3. Are you curious about the significance of 29 statements?
4. If not, did you circle 24C?
5. Did you have a hard time choosing one letter for each number?
6. Did you find any statements where none of the letters applied?
7. Was there a part about choosing just one?
8. What rules have you created for yourself that limit you?
9. If you could be known for just one thing, what would that be?

Answers:

1. Give yourself 9 bonus points for going back to that tediously important exercise.
2. As humans we have an innate desire to look for and find patterns. Although there were no patterns that I could come up with, if you found any patterns, contact us[47], reveal your findings, and you could win a prize.
3. Although the statements were numbered to twenty-eight, there were actually twenty-nine statements. Twenty-nine is one of the more attractive prime numbers, it's the atomic number of copper, it has a lot of biblical significance (but what number doesn't, really?), it represents the number of years it takes Saturn to orbit our sun, and some numerologists claim that it's related to relationships and diplomacy. Cool.
4. That was the one about not being...observant.
5. Why choose just one? It's not fattening to define what you're not.
6. There were probably statements where none of the letters applied. That information is useful too.
7. Nope. No rule.
8. You gotta answer this one: What rules have you created for yourself that limit you? Here's one my son just suggested: choosing to continue the childhood rule of not talking to strangers limits your connections.
9. Only you can say what you want to be known for. If I had to pick it for you, it would be...inventing and making me a thigh-firming pineapple upside-down cake. I'm not good at dreaming for others.

Exercise 6.6: Secret Bonus (A Tool for Overachievers)
Curiosity killers are everywhere. In our age of data deluge and instant access to information, the barrier for something to qualify as a study, an expert opinion, research, or science is just too low to allow those claims to stifle our curiosity about the claim. That makes not being curious very dangerous.

You can crush curiosity killers. Here's how.

1. Identify the curiosity killers—the authoritative sources that seduce us into blindly believing the claim that follows. These anchor us to believability. Here are a few to watch out for:
   - According to experts...
   - Studies show...
   - Research indicates...
   - Science says...
   - It's a known fact that...
2. Disarm the curiosity killers and elevate your curiosity by asking these simple questions:
   - Compared to what?
   - As measured by what?
   - Conducted by whom?
   - Tested on what?
   - Am I being tricked into thinking correlation is causation. You know, that trick that makes it seem like just because two items are correlated, one caused the other?
   - Is this bogus to begin with?

Remember that living curiously is not about endless inquiry. It is about being curiously vigilant about knowing enough to make better decisions, solve problems, and live a more fulfilling and adventurous life.

Conclusion

My sister and I were enjoying perfect quantities of fine Nicaraguan rum while swaying to the reggae and calypso music, breathing the sweet ganja-filled air, and listening to the cacophony of languages from around the world. Puerto Viejo, Costa Rica, provided the mixture of Caribbean and indigenous Bribri culture that we were seeking. The Mango Sunset Bar provided just the right setting for one of my favorite living curiously activities: sitting with my sister, Jennifer, at a slightly crowded bar with twinkling lights bouncing off glass bottles, enticing boozy concoctions, and cross-pollinating opportunities with fellow bar mates. Except for the cool addition of a hovering sloth and scampering lizards, this living curiously bar experience was pretty typical.

Jennifer and I had pulled up to the bar in a rickety golf cart. Although our search for howler monkeys and caimans earlier in the day may have been easier on foot, the golf cart bouncing precariously down the gravel road while navigating crater-size potholes provided more opportunity to have fun...and to be ridiculous. It was not our goal to be obnoxious Americans, but humor is one of the fun ways that my sister and I connect with others when traveling. When the teenage boy suggested we rent his cart, we surprised him by saying what we usually say when offered a chance to humiliate ourselves: "Sure."

By the time we walked into the bar, our future bar mates had seen our pathetic attempt to park the cart. They were all already laughing at us...all except for a quiet guy with impressive dreadlocks at the end of the bar.

We curiously engaged our fellow world travelers. They shared stories of their amazing adventures and readily competed with stories of scary near misses. Ashley had lived in a remote village in Ivory Coast and later had met her girlfriend in Nepal. Itamar pitted his story of accidentally wandering into a crowd of gun-toting revolutionaries in South America against Jorge's story of getting stranded without supplies by a washed-out road in the Philippines. There was a generous amount of pity tossed about for those who don't experience the adventure of world travel.

As usual, we learned new things and fantasized about the enticing invitations to join travel adventures. But I was particularly curious about that quiet, dreadlocked guy at the end of the bar.

And so I bought him a drink.

At first he seemed skeptical—like he was encountering an older woman (which he was) whose intentions were unclear (which I quickly cleared up). I left the group, scooted next to him, and explained that I was working on a Living Curiously project and wanted to know if I could ask him a few questions. He quietly agreed, so I asked him, "What did your childhood smell like?"

It was clear that he heard me and thought it was a weird question. It was also clear that it aroused his curiosity and he was really thinking about the answer. It was a long four minutes before he responded, "It smelled like dis."

"Like...ganja and rum?" I asked him.

"Yeah, sort of. And the other smells too. I was born and raised here, so that makes sense."

"Cool. What do you think would be most surprising about what it's like to be born and raised here?"

Another long pause.

"I come to dis bar to notice. I have learned a lot about places I will probably never be able to visit. I don't think it's different here than all the places they talk about going. All those places they go and people they meet can become so familiar that they are no longer...fascinating. I might not be able to travel—not like many of them anyway. That doesn't make me someone who misses out...unless I let it. Earlier, I noticed you and your friend bumping around on that golf cart."

"Yeah, that's my sister."

"You laugh a lot. I have never even tried dat crazy. I should. I got to stay curious."

That's it! You may recognize what my dreadlock-y friend was describing—elevating curiosity to find the mystique in the mundane. However, before that moment I had not really understood the concept as clearly. That conversation made me glad we'd said, "Sure," to the golf cart and embraced the hilarity-loving, middle-aged Americans that we are. It also refocused my attention on staying curious when familiarity threatens to squash fascination. That conversation, like so many other curious conversations, changed my life.

Living curiously will affect all the areas of your life. For most people, the greatest impact of living curiously is how it creates a more adventurous life and how it helps solve problems and make better decisions. By now you understand how these benefits often mush together.

...

As you start to tally up your bonus points and this book draws to a close, toast your astonishingly curious self. From this day forward, and for the rest of your life, you will be filled with more insights and greater adventure. You will see things that others miss. And, because it's the best magic trick for your life, you'll continue to elevate curiosity. That's really good for you, but because you have the Method as your framework for using curiosity to be remarkable and do good stuff, it will also be massively good for the world. Become a force for helping others to elevate curiosity, and you'll help create a tribe of curiosity seekers that can revolutionize how we see, experience, and benefit the world.

Elevate curiosity and use it well.

Resources

Curious about How to Get Help?

Jump over to www.LivingCuriously.net.

Check out the Living Curiously Method Workbooks and other Living Curiously learning opportunities at www.LivingCuriously.net.

Check out the *Curiosity Hacks* ebooks at www.LivingCuriously.net.

Contact me about speaking at your next event: www.BeckiSaltzman.com/speaker.

Curious about How You Can Help?

We are training and certifying a few select Living Curiously Coaches. Think you'd like to help and inspire others? Hit us up, and we'll send you an application for our Living Curiously Coaching Certification program (availability is limited).

Contact us if you're interested in hosting a Living Curiously event in your hometown.

Let's Meet Soon

Living Curiously was never meant to stand alone as a book you read once in solitary confinement, but there are plans to gift it to several particularly curious inmates. The Method is meant to be chewed, used, discussed, and shared. But don't swallow—approach it with curiosity bordering on skepticism. It is meant to help jump-start the discovery of a curious way of making sense of the world. I'd love to be a part of your remarkable life, so please don't be a stranger. Cross-pollinate with me at www.LivingCuriously.net.

Really Great Reading

I love books. This list could go on and on, but here's a bunch of books that I have enjoyed. These represent a cross-pollination of ideas and perspectives. I guarantee that applying curiosity while reading these books will change your life in profoundly good ways.

The $12 Million Stuffed Shark: The Curious Economics of Contemporary Art
> By Don Thompson
> Why? If you're curious about the enormous and mostly un-regulated economic market and the strange world of contemporary art, this book is a fascinating exposé.

Africans on Stage: Studies in Ethnological Show Business
> Edited by Bernth Lindfors
> Why? If you're curious about how human beings have been treated like objects for entertainment and about how disgusting yourself with history may disgust you out of complacency, this book can help.

Arousing the Buy Curious: Real Estate Pillow Talk for Patrons and Professionals
> By Becki Saltzman
> Why? If you're curious about real estate and the secrets that make real estate transactions more successful, this book may be the best real estate investment you can make.

The Artist's Way
> By Julia Cameron
> Why? If you're curious about a twelve-week program that has been used by an uncountable number of artists to ignite their creativity, this book may work for you too.

The Black Swan: The Impact of the Highly Improbable
> By Nassim Nicholas Taleb
> Why? If you're curious about highly unlikely, rare, and unpredictable events that have massive impact, this book will

help you to see these sneaky events coming before anyone else does (as long as they haven't read the book).

The Complete Hans Christian Andersen Fairy Tales
Edited by Lily Owens
Why? If you're curious about the lessons that hide in our cherished fables like "The Snow Queen," "The Ugly Duckling," and "The Emperor's New Clothes," you may surprise yourself by how much you'll enjoy reading this.

Confessions of an Advertising Man
By David Ogilvy
Why? If you're curious about advertising, this is the seminal book about the subject, from the man who elevated the advertising agency business from reselling ad space to creating and pitching like a madman and to the relatively less boozy profession it has become.

The Critical Thinker's Dictionary: Biases, Fallacies, and Illusions and What You Can Do about Them
By Robert Todd Carroll
Why? If you're curious about how to avoid being deceived by your own brain...or the brains of others, this will reveal the deceptions and help you avoid them.

Diagnostic and Statistical Manual of Mental Disorders, Fifth Edition
By American Psychiatric Association
Why? If you're curious about what doctors, politicians, pharmaceutical companies, and insurance companies were able to pull together as the current gospel on mental disorders, you may find this manual fun to compare with earlier editions.

Ebola, Culture, and Politics: The Anthropology of an Emerging Disease
By Barry S. Hewlett, Bonnie L. Hewlett
Why? If you're curious about doing good stuff involving aid work abroad (and you're patient enough to read an academic book), this anthropologist's view of the Ebola

eradication efforts will help you understand why it's critically important to elevate curiosity.

Future Babble: Why Expert Predictions are Next to Worthless and You Can Do Better
By Dan Gardner
Why? If you're curious about the future, this book will help you realize that you shouldn't bother with the meaningless predictions of the experts. You can do better predicting for yourself.

Harry Potter and the Sorcerer's Stone
By J. K. Rowling
Why? If you're curious about the kind of magic that is required to appeal to the broadest range of human readers, this book will make you wish you were a wizard.

The Hour: A Cocktail Manifesto
By Bernard DeVoto
Why? If you're curious about booze, this is the classic written before mixology was a thing, by a historian, scholar, novelist, Mark Twain aficionado, and lover of whisky and the martini. Rum lovers may be ridiculed.

How Music Works
By David Byrne
Why? If you're curious about music, let this author, painter, philosopher, film and record producer, and lead singer of Talking Heads be your industry tour guide.

How Soccer Explains the World: An Unlikely Theory of Globalization
By Franklin Foer
Why? If you're curious about soccer and how it affects the global economy, politics, and life, this book will give you insights that will delight and surprise you. Feel free to think about the effects of other sports.

I Am America (And So Can You!)
> By Stephen Colbert
>
> Why? If you're curious about 'merica and savvy satire, this book should not be read in a quiet place unless you're better than I am at stifling laughter.

If... (Questions for the Game of Life)
> By Evelyn McFarlane and James Saywell
>
> Why? If you're curious about fun and provocative questions that can turn long commutes and boring dinner guests into fun and cringeworthy times, start the If series with this book.

Influence: The Psychology of Persuasion
> By Robert B. Cialdini
>
> Why? If you're curious about how to achieve anything in a world where you have to live among and convince other humans, this book will show you science behind how to do it.

The Innovator's Solution: Creating and Sustaining Successful Growth
> By Clayton M. Christensen and Michael E. Raynor
>
> Why? If you're curious about the overused word *disruption*, this book will reveal what that word meant when it was first unleashed on the buzzword-loving business world.

Islam and the Future of Tolerance
> By Sam Harris and Maajid Nawaz
>
> Why? If you're curious about understanding key issues around religion, reform, and Islam in the modern world, this brilliant and civil dialogue will inform and enlighten you.

Kitchen Confidential: Adventures in the Culinary Underbelly
> By Anthony Bourdain
>
> Why? If you're curious about the underbelly of the restaurant world and what goes on behind what goes into your gullet, these horror stories will entertain while possibly giving you more than a kitchen crush on Anthony Bourdain.

Me Talk Pretty One Day
  By David Sedaris
  Why? If you're curious about why learning French is hard and why David Sedaris is hilarious, this book about David dealing with life and trying to learn French will make you laugh out loud and it will whet your appetite for more of David's books.

Memoirs of the Second World War
  By Winston S. Churchill
  Why? If you're curious about the guy who said, "Success is not final, failure is not fatal; it is the courage to continue that counts," you will enjoy this firsthand account of the Second World War from this Nobel Prize winner in literature.

Naked, Drunk, and Writing: Shed Your Inhibitions and Craft a Compelling Memoir or Personal Essay
  By Adair Lara
  Why? If you're curious about being a writer, this great writing book is best read with booze or without underwear.

Plato and a Platypus Walk into a Bar: Understanding Philosophy Through Jokes
  By Thomas Cathcart and Daniel Klein
  Why? If you're curious about profound philosophers and world philosophies, having them hilariously explained makes them easier to understand. You'll be the hit at any event ending with the word *gala*.

Predictably Irrational: The Hidden Forces That Shape Our Decisions
  By Dan Ariely
  Why? If you're curious about the decisions we make, this book reveals how we predictably make irrational decisions. Maybe this will help us to not make such dumb decisions anymore.

The Principles of Uncertainty
   By Maira Kalman
   Why? If you're curious about what to buy for your friend who
      appreciates hard-to-define, thought-provoking stuff and
      art, sociology, philosophy, and travel, this book will be a
      perfect gift that you should borrow from her.

*Race: How Blacks and Whites Think and Feel About the American
Obsession*
   By Studs Terkel
   Why? If you're curious about race relations in America, what
      this master interviewer was able to uncover will give you
      a candid glimpse at the early nineties...and goose bumps.

The Righteous Mind: Why Good People Are Divided by Politics and Religion
   By Jonathan Haidt
   Why? If you're curious about cocktail-party-taboo topics like
      atheism and religion, liberals and conservatives, good and
      evil, and morality, this book explains why we're so divided.
      Perhaps it will help us be better to one another.

*The Spirit Catches You and You Fall Down: A Hmong Child, Her
American Doctors, and the Collision of Two Cultures*
   By Anne Fadiman
   Why? If you're curious about vast cultural challenges when
      American medical technology meets ancient Eastern cul-
      ture, this riveting book about a particularly tragic event in
      a Hmong community will blow your mind...and stay with
      you until you fall down for the last time.

Thinking, Fast and Slow
   By Daniel Kahneman
   Why? If you're curious about how we think and you think
      thinking matters, this is the best or second best book that
      can help you think smarter.

The Way I Am
    By Eminem
    Why? If you're curious about how a rapper might put together
        a very creative storybook of reflections, lyrics, drawings,
        and photographs, this is a glorious example.

Check Out This Good Stuff

In addition to the various remarkable folks who were highlighted
in this book, there are many others who were also a significant
part of this living curiously adventure. Here's a tiny sampling of
the good stuff that inspired this book:

www.AltaPlanning.com
www.ArtByDino.com
www.bjfogg.com
www.BrainBlogger.com
www.criticalthinking.org
www.CompassionAndChoices.org
www.danariely.com/the-research
www.DinoDesign-O.com
www.DutchBros.com
www.freakonomics.com
www.IdeaLiftoff.com
www.InfluenceAtWork.com
www.ThePongoFund.org
www.procon.org
www.RivetedLife.com
www.sjdm.org
www.Skeptic.com

Additional Sources

If you've been curious about my sources, I've included endnotes throughout the book just for you. A few more sources informed the foundation of this book, so they're not married to any one particular place to attach a note. I list them here for your reference:

Kashdan, T. B., and M. F. Steger. "Curiosity and Pathways to Well-Being and Meaning in Life: Traits, States, and Everyday Behaviors," *Motivation and Emotion* 31, no. 3 (2007): 159–73.

Loewenstein, G. "The Psychology of Curiosity: A Review and Reinterpretation," *Psychological Bulletin* 116, no. 1 (1994): 75–98.

Reio, T. G., Jr., and A. Wiswell. "Field Investigation of the Relationship among Adult Curiosity, Workplace Learning, and Job Performance," *Human Resource Development Quarterly* 11, no. 1 (2001): 5–30.

Swan, G. E., and D. Carmelli. "Curiosity and Mortality in Aging Adults: A 5-Year Follow-Up of the Western Collaborative Group Study," *Psychology and Aging* 11, no. 3 (1996): 449–53.

von Stumm, S., B. Hell, and T. Chamorro-Premuzic. "The Hungry Mind: Intellectual Curiosity Is the Third Pillar of Academic Performance," *Perspectives on Psychological Science* 6, no. 6 (2011): 574–88.

Appreciation

E very time I start this appreciation section of *Living Curiously*,
I feel overwhelmed with gratitude...and scared shitless that
I am going to leave out many of the people who have been remarkable influences in my life. If you think, *Hey, I remember when
we talked about curiosity at the coffee shop*, I'm talking about you. If
you think, *I endured those crazy curious questions*, know that this
appreciation section is here because of you.

I'm thankful for my family. We are an unconventional lot.
My husband, Stephen, is one of the most curious people I know.
I rarely catch him glancing at his device when he tires of the
fact that I find confrontation a sport almost as enjoyable as he
finds entrepreneurship, the Oregon Ducks, and soccer. My son
Barkley is hilarious and helped me apply skepticism and analysis
to studies without too much cynicism. My son Dane entertained
me with rap battles and helped me explain complicated ideas in
simply smarter ways (where I failed, it was probably because I
didn't listen to him). My sister, Jennifer, helped test the Method
during adventures near and far. I am grateful for my brother, Jeff,
who showcases the value of elevating curiosity when debating
subjects we may or may not agree on. As my amazing audiobook
recording engineer, my brother-in-law, Sony, sat with me for
hours. I'm grateful for my hilarious and supportive dad, Bob,
who along with my late and sparkly mom, Carol, caused my curiosity disorder. I am grateful for Ruth, the best and most curious
mother-in-law in the land. My scrumptious grandma, Alice, has
applied her editorial prowess and nearly one hundred years of
living curiously to these pages. I'm grateful to and for her.

Thank you to Dino Paul, Joanne McCall, Ali Shaw, Vinnie Kinsella, Tina Granzo, Jim Parker, Sue Surdam, Guillaume Schaer, Shane Cameron, Jeremy Salsbury, Patrick Cummings, Laura Fravel, Joanna Miller, Irv Potter, Kohel Haver, Karry Price, and Motti Wilhelm, Patty McNally, Paul Wild, Janna Lopez, Marty Mianji.

Over the years, little tidbits of understanding acquired from serendipitous interactions have combined with mind-blowing insights from structured interviews and research. It's hard to measure the unique impact of any of these, and I'm not sure I would want to. I am grateful beyond words for all of these people and experiences.

About the Author

Becki Saltzman is a curiosity consultant, assumption buster, and idea generator. She holds a master's degree in behavioral science from Washington University in Saint Louis and has spent the last two decades studying curiosity and the role it plays in adventure and insights, problem solving and idea generation, sales and ideal lifestyle design.

She is the author of *Arousing the Buy Curious: Real Estate Pillow Talk for Patrons and Professionals* and is a blogger and columnist, professional speaker, ex–real estate broker and fashion buyer, and the host of *What Are You Missing? A Podcast of Living Curiously*.

Becki is the founder of the Living Curiously Lifestyle and creator of the Living Curiously Method—a framework and teaching program for using curiosity to accomplish remarkable things in adventure, work, and life. She is the spawn of master persuader auctioneers and the breeder of boys. When not traveling to speak about curiosity and living curiously, she lives in Portland, Oregon, with her husband and two sons. She loves great travel adventures, crowded dance floors, and brown drinks.

Becki invites you to join the Tribe of the Curious at BeckiSaltzman.com.

Endnotes

1. Check out www.wikipedia.org/wiki/Tikkun_olam to satisfy your curiosity.
2. Philip Ball, *Curiosity: How Science Became Interested in Everything* (Chicago: University of Chicago Press, 2014). And *Monty Python and the Holy Grail.*
3. Wolfe Mays, "Scientific Method in Galileo and Bacon," *Indian Philosophical Quarterly* 1 (1974): 217–239, www.unipune.ac.in /snc/cssh/ipq/english/IPQ/1-5 volumes/01-3/1-3-3.pdf.
4. See www.royalsociety.org/about-us/history.
5. See www.en.wikipedia.org/wiki/Movement_for_the_ Restoration_of_the_Ten_Commandments_of_God.
6. See www.en.wikipedia.org/wiki/Family_International.
7. George Loewenstein, "The Psychology of Curiosity: A Review and Reinterpretation," *Psychological Bulletin* 116, no.1 (1994): 75–98, www.cmu.edu/dietrich/sds/docs/loewen stein/PsychofCuriosity.pdf.
8. D. E. Berlyne, "Curiosity and Exploration," Science 153, no. 3731 (1966): 25–33; and Loewenstein, "Psychology of Curiosity."
9. Russel Golman and George Loewenstein, "Curiosity, Information Gaps, and the Utility of Knowledge," Social Science Research Network (March 30, 2014), http://ssrn.com /abstract=2149362.
10. Susannah Cahalan, *Brain on Fire: My Month of Madness* (New York: Simon & Schuster, 2013).
11. See www.cell.com/neuron/abstract/S0896-6273%2814% 2900804-6.

12. You can order my book at wwwArousingTheBuyCurious.com.

13. Daniel Kahneman, Thinking, Fast and Slow (New York: Farrar, Straus and Giroux, 2013), 12.

14. Join up at www.BeckiSaltzman.com/join-the-tribe-of-the -curious.

15. Leonid Rozenblit and Frank Keil, "The Misunderstood Limits of Folk Science: An Illusion of Explanatory Depth," Cognitive Science 26, no. 5 (2002): 521–62.

16. See www.wikipedia.org/wiki/Tehuelche_language.

17. Robert B. Cialdini, Influence: The Psychology of Persuasion (New York: Harper Business, 2006).

18. See www.dutchbros.com/AboutUs.

19. Wendy Culverwell, "How Dutch Bros. Grew from a Pushcart in Grants Pass to a $150M Coffee Mainstay," Portland Business Journal, August 14, 2014, www.bizjournals.com /portland/blog/2014/08/how-dutch-bros-grew-from-a-push cart-in-grants-pass.html?page=all.

20. See www.wikipedia.org/wiki/Barnum_effect.

21. Kathy Pezdek and Matthew Prull, "Fallacies in Memory for Conversations: Reflections on Clarence Thomas, Anita Hill, and the Like," Applied Cognitive Psychology 7, no. 4 (1993): 299–310.

22. David H. Hsu and Kwanghui Lim, "Knowledge Brokering and Organizational Innovation: Founder Imprinting Effects," Organization Science 25, no. 4 (2014): 1134–53, www.dx.doi .org/10.1287/orsc.2013.0863.

23. Andrew Hargadon and Robert I. Sutton, "Technology Brokering and Innovation in a Product Development Firm," Administrative Science Quarterly 42, no. 4 (1997): 716–49.

24. Andrew Hargadon, How Breakthroughs Happen: The Surprising Truth about How Companies Innovate (Boston: Harvard Business Review Press, 2003).

25. Lee Fleming, "Perfecting Cross-Pollination," Harvard Business Review, September 2004, www.hbr.org/2004/09 /perfecting-cross-pollination/ar/1.

26. See www.wikipedia.org/wiki/Iconoclasm.

27. David Hume, An Enquiry Concerning Human Understanding (Oxford: Oxford University Press, [1748] 2007).

28. Reid Wilson, *Don't Panic: Taking Control of Anxiety Attacks*, 3rd ed. (New York: Harper Perennial, 2009).

29. Adam Galinsky et al., "Why It Pays to Get Inside the Head of Your Opponent: The Differential Effects of Perspective Taking and Empathy in Negotiations," *Psychological Science* 19, no. 4 (2008): 378–84.

30. Nicholas A. Christakis and James H. Fowler, "The Spread of Obesity in a Large Social Network Over 32 Years," *New England Journal of Medicine* 357, no. 4 (2007): 370–79; ———, "Quitting in Droves: Collective Dynamics of Smoking Behavior in a Large Social Network," *New England Journal of Medicine* 358, no. 21 (2008): 2249–58; http://link.springer.com/article/10.1007/s10902-005-1915-1#page-2; and Christakos and Fowler, "Social Network Sensors for Early Detection of Contagious Outbreaks," PLoS ONE 5, no. 9 (2010): e12948.

31. See www.McCallMediaGroup.com.

32. Randy Garner, "What's in a Name? Persuasion Perhaps," *Journal of Consumer Psychology* 15, no. 2(2005): 108–16; and Cialdini, *Influence*, 173–74.

33. See www.IdeaLiftOff.com.

34. Cialdini, *Influence*; and Dennis T. Regan, "Effects of a Favor and Liking on Compliance," *Journal of Experimental Social Psychology* 7 (1971): 627–39; and Shelly Chaiken, "Heuristic versus Systematic Information Processing and the Use of Source versus Message Cues in Persuasion," *Journal of Personality and Social Psychology*, 39, no. 5 (1980): 752–66.

35. Ernst Fehr and Simon Gächter, "Fairness and Retaliation: The Economics of Reciprocity," *The Journal of Economic Perspectives* 14, no. 3 (2000), 159–81; and Robert B. Cialdini et al., "Reciprocal Concessions Procedure for Inducing Compliance: The Door-in-the-Face Technique," *Journal of Personality and Social Psychology* 31, no. 2 (1975), 206–15.

36. Noah J. Goldstein, Robert B. Cialdini, and Vladas Griskevicius, "A Room with a Viewpoint: Using Social Norms to Motivate Environmental Conservation in Hotels," *Journal of Consumer Research* 35 (2008): 472–82.

37. Delia Cioffi and Randy Garner, "On Doing the Decision: Effects of Active versus Passive Choice on Commitment and

Self-Perception," *Personality and Social Psychology Bulletin* 22, no. 2 (1996): 133–47.

38. Amos Tversky and Daniel Kahneman, "Loss Aversion in Riskless Choice: A Reference-Dependent Model," *The Quarterly Journal of Economics* 106, no. 4 (1991): 1039–61.

39. Mike Wall, "The Moon and Man at 50: Why JFK's Space Exploration Speech Still Resonates," *Space.com*, May 25, 2011, www.space.com/11774-jfk-speech-moon-exploration-ken nedy-congress-50years.html.

40. "Project Apollo: A Retrospective Analysis," NASA, last modified April 21, 2014, www.history.nasa.gov/Apollomon/Apollo. html; "May 25, 1961: JFK's Moon Shot Speech to Congress," *Space.com*, May 25, 2011, www.space.com/11772-president -kennedy-historic-speech-moon-space.html.

41. Marcus Lindroos, "The Cost of the Moon Race: $100 Billion to Land on the Moon," *The Artemis Project*, last updated November 4, 1997, www.asi.org/adb/m/02/07/apollo-cost.html.

42. See https://spinoff.nasa.gov/apollo.htm.

43. "Death of the Double Irish," *The Economist*, October 15, 2014, www.economist.com/news/business-and-finance/21625444 -irish-government-has-announced-plans-alter-one-its-more -controversial-tax-policies.

44. Jeffrey L. Rubinger and Summer Ayers Lepree, "Death of the 'Double Irish Dutch Sandwich'? Not So Fast," *Taxes without Borders*, October 23, 2014, www.taxeswithoutbordersblog .com/2014/10/death-of-the-double-irish-dutch-sandwich -not-so-fast.

45. Jihae Shin and Katherine L. Milkman, "Can Preparing for Failure Reduce the Probability of Success?" (lecture, Society for Judgment and Decision Making, 2014 35th Annual Conference, Long Beach, CA, November 23, 2014).

46. Ting Zhang et al., "A 'Present' for the Future: The Unexpected Value of Rediscovery," *Psychological Science* (August 29, 2014).

47. Contact us at www.BeckiSaltzman.com/contact.

CPSIA information can be obtained
at www.ICGtesting.com
Printed in the USA
LVOW01s2011160217

524489LV00029B/641/P